The
HOUR of MEETING
EVIL SPIRITS

an Encyclopedia of Mononoke and Magic

written and illustrated
by
MATTHEW MEYER

ISBN-10:0-9852184-3-6
ISBN-13: 978-0-9852184-3-0

www.matthewmeyer.net
www.yokai.com

This book is dedicated to my wife, who is my favorite yōkai of all, and to all of the fans who supported my second Kickstarter project.

A. L. Koehl, Aaron Dilliplane, Aaron W. Thorne, Adam Buckheit, Adam Ef, Al Billings, Albert Lew, Albert Martinez, Albert Tsang, Alberto M., Alex Johnson, Alex T Guerrero, Alexander "Guddha" Gudenau, Alexander Brown, Alexander Lucard, Allen Sorensen, Alvin Leung, Amorita Malagon, AndLiew, Andreas Hamm, Andrew Clough, Andrew Lohmann, Andrew Talarico, Andy K, Angelia Pitman, Angelique Blansett, Anthony Catino, Antoine aka Illyan, Antonio Vincentelli, Antti Hallamäki, Antti Luukkonen, aoife and ryan, April Gutierrez, Ariel Mei Roberts, Arnold Cassell, Ash Brown, Bambu, Barac Wiley, Barry E. Moore, Bel Tomov, Ben W Bell, Benjamin Daws, Benjamin Fox, Brad Gabriel, Brad Mushill, Brandon Hall, Bredon Clay, Brett Slocum, Brian "Fitz" Fitzpatrick, Brian Dysart, Brian Sulz, Brianne Bedard, Brigitte Colbert, Bronwen Everill, Brook West, Camellia Samir El-Antably, Cameron Gehlert, Campbell Ruddock, Cara Terry, Carlo Bottiglieri, Carlos Zermeño, Carter Allen, Caspian Moore, CHAMP WU, Chandra "Ritsuna" Graham, Charles Liao, Chen X. Chen, Cheryl Costella, Chris Hales, Chris Mihal, Chris Olsen, Christina M Hughes, Christopher, Claire MacPherson, Clark and Carrol, Contento Anthony, Corey M. Modrowski, Courts Casswell Towns, Craig S. Weinstein, Cudinski Family, Curt sherman, Cynthia Pierce, D. P. Rider, Damien Hunter, Damon-Eugene Rich, Daniel B. Nissman, Daniel Joseph Tavares Moore, Daniel Stein, David G Barnes, David Inacio, David Rubenach, Dawn Oshima, Deborah Spiesz, Debra Dickinson, Dennis Hougaard Boje, Derek Gutrath, Dimitri Widroiajegodomitcher, Dion C. Perez, Doskoi Panda, Doug Sarver, Dr Paul Dale, Drew (Andrew) South, Dylan Boates, E.L. Winberry, Eden Brandeis, Edouard Foraz, Elliott Sawyer, elRoy, Eric Bertish, Eric Zylstra, Erik & Anna Meyer, Erik Norman Berglund, Filip Källman, "Filkertom" Tom Smith, Forrest Service, Frances McGregor, Frank Laycock, Gary and Sandra Meyer, Gary Gaines, Gary Lau, Gary Tanigawa, GC Lim, Gilbert Pettingell, Glenn McLean, Gordon Garb, Grant Voakes, Greg Zuro, Guilherme Reis Bonfim, Gwen Sato-Herrick, H Lynnea Johnson, H. Hrubey, Hayley G. Hofmar-Glennon, Heather Blandford, Heather Hintze, Heidi Ellis, Helena Alves, HIROAKI KAMIDATE, Hitomi Meyer, Ilsa Enomoto, Imran Inayat, India Swift, Ingmar, Iris Mei Cooper Ingham, Iso Stein, Israel Cortes, Ivy Antunes, J Schultz, J,A,E Yip, Jaap Kreijkamp, Jacob Dylan Riddle, Jacob E. Boucher, Jacqueline Skelton, Jai Goggan aka. J-Ace, Jak Butanabe, Jakob Asbury, Jakob Frederiksen, James and Julia Ford, James Edward Johnson, Jamie Taylor, Janna Solis, Jason Aaron Wong & The Wong Family, Jason Koivu, Javier Aparicio Ferrer, Jeff M, Jeff Siegel, Jeff Sweeney, Jeffrey Friesen, Jeffrey Peralta, Jen B, JF Garrard, John, john guthrie, John Merklinghaus, John Santagada, John William Bass, Jon C, Jonathan Cabildo, Jonathan Jacobs, Jorge L, Jose Luis Equiza, Josh Haycraft, Josh Scott, Joshua Beale, Joshua W. Pittman, Juha-Pekka Pulkkinen, Julia B. Ellingboe, Julian Chan, Jussi Myllyluoma, Justin Varney, Kali Lynn, Karla Steffen, Karon Flage, Karra L., Kat Nakaji, Kathryn Blue, Katy Richard, Kay James, Kay M, Kazumi Teune, Kelly Lowrey, Ken T., Kenji Ishii, Kenny Loh, Kenton and Paula Meyer, Kerwell, Kira Graham, Knurenko Veronika, Krista Hoxie, Kristian Jansen Jaech, KuwaNeko, Kyle McLauchlan, Larry Lade, Lars Ericson, Laurel S, Leo Hourvitz, Leonard Kim, Leora Effinger-Weintraub, Leslie Barrett Beck, Lexi Akemi, Lin Zhou, Lisa Kaiffer, M. H. Boroson, Maggie Griffeth, Maggie Young, Marie Mint, Mark Franklin, Mark Gieringer, Mark Terrano, Mark Wilko, Markus Ullrich, Mary Kathryn Hammond, Mary Prince, Masako Castile, Matt Erik Katch, Matthew Benson, Matthew Higgins, Matthew Hochberg, Mauro Ghibaudo, Max Kaehn, Maximilian Hoetzl, Mendel Schmiedekamp, Michael "Kyoflamez" Bridgemohan, Michael Brandon Jones, Michael Brewer, Michael Cammarata, Michael D. Blanchard, Mike (kirstgrafx) Lee, Mike Pallas, Mike Urano, Mikkel "Hobbosnorken" Keilhau, Mira Solmeyer, Mitchell Olson, Mon Geslani, Mr. & Mrs. Charles Don Hall, Ms. Annie Nohn, Nathan Olmstead, Nathan Seabolt, Nathan Smyth, Nick Tantra, Nikki Tran, Noriko & Hiroto Ichihashi, Occams Electric Toothbrush, Olai Amund, Olna Jenn Smith, Pablo Rambla, Patrick Donoghue, Patrick Lipo, Patrick Tan Wei Ming, Patty Kirsch, Patty Mitchell, Paul Gorman, Paul Hachmann, Paul T Smith, Paul Thorgrimson, Penchour, Peter Li, Peter Riordan, Peter, Emma, Gabriella and Emilia Rossi, Petter Wäss, PnutBandit, Polly Whitmore, porusan, Rachael Hixon, Raphaela Cologna , Rebecca Mutton, Reid Hirata, Revek, Reverance Pavane, Richard and Cheryl Everill, Rob Chow, Robert & Linda Hewitt, Robert E. Stutts, Robert Farley, Robert Lee Mayers, Robert Richard Franke III, Robin, Rommy Driks, Rufus, Ryan Yoo, S.Y. Inamura, Sabina Kneisly, Samantha Balyeat, Samuel Coudry-Lemay, Sangha Farms, Sarah Joan Christensen, Scanner@apricot.com, Scott A. Harrison, Scott Richardson, Sean Holland, SEM, Shane Williamson, Shayna Harris, Shean, Semeicha and Sapphira Mohammed, Sheila Mazur, Shermaine Nicole A. Garcia, Sian Nelson, Simone D. Bennett, Stef Maruch, Stefan Wagner, Stefanie Kreutzer, Steph Turner, Stephanie Wagner, Stephen A. Caldwell, Stephen Hazlewood, Stephen Hill, Stephen I., Stephen Shiu, Steve Jasper, Steven Moy, Stewart Falconer, Stuart Martin, Susan Patrick, T.S. Luikart, tagno25, Talon Johnson, Tatiana Alejandra de Castro Pérez, Tenkai, Tereza Kulovaná, Tetsuko Toda, The Bhoo, The Reiters of Haddonfield, Thorjw, Thuy Nguyen, Tim Elrod, Toast Peters, Tom Phillips, Tony Love and family, Toshimitsu & Mikiko Umeda, Tury G, Universe Frog, Vaughan Monnes, Victoria E.S. Pullen, Vintson Knight, Wm. Ellery Samuels, Ph.D., Xiaocheng (Jack) Shi, Yawei, Yoshiko Sawai, Youkai Lonely Hearts Society

CONTENTS

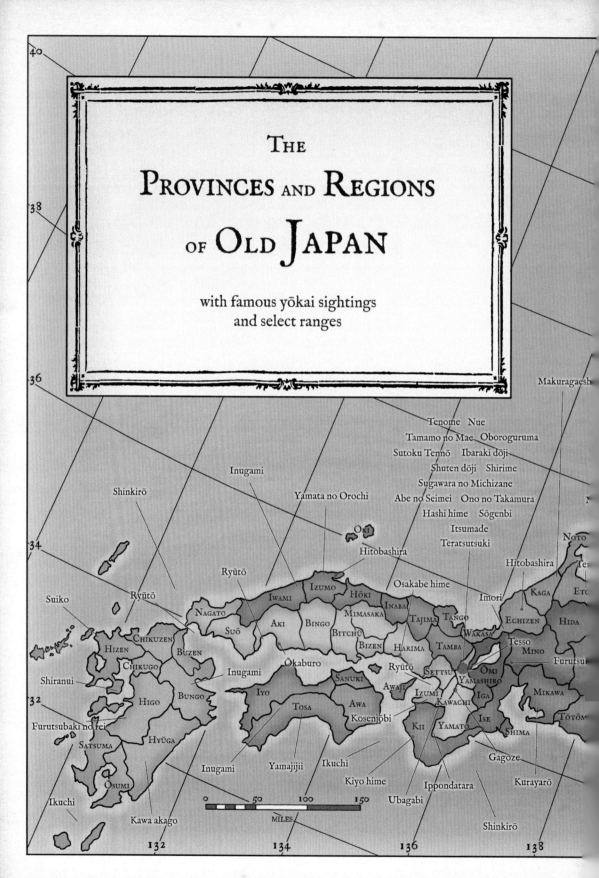

THE
PROVINCES AND REGIONS
OF OLD JAPAN

with famous yōkai sightings
and select ranges

40

38

36

34

32

Makuragaesh

Tenome   Nue
Tamamo no Mae   Oboroguruma
Sutoku Tennō   Ibaraki dōji
Shuten dōji   Shirime
Sugawara no Michizane
Abe no Seimei   Ono no Takamura
Hashi hime   Sōgenbi
Itsumade
Teratsutsuki

Inugami

Shinkirō

Yamata no Orochi

Oki

Hitobashira

NOTO

Hitobashira

Te

Ryūtō

IZUMO   HŌKI

Osakabe hime

Imori

KAGA   ETC

Ryūtō

IWAMI

MIMASAKA

INABA

TAJIMA   TANGO

ECHIZEN   HIDA

Suiko

NAGATO

AKI   BINGO

BITCHŪ

WAKASA

Tesso

SUŌ

BIZEN

HARIMA   TAMBA

MINO

CHIKUZEN

Furutsu

HIZEN   BUZEN

Ōkaburo

Ryūtō

SETTSU   ŌMI

CHIKUGO

Inugami

SANUKI

AWAJI   IZUMI   KAWACHI   IGA

MIKAWA

Shiranui

IYO

AWA   Kosenjōbi

YAMASHIRO

HIGO   BUNGO

TOSA

ISE

TŌTŌM

32

Furutsubaki no rei

KII   YAMATO

SHIMA

SATSUMA

HYŪGA

Inugami

Yamajijii

Ikuchi

Gagōze

Ippondatara

Kurayarō

Ikuchi

ŌSUMI

Kiyo hime

Ubagabi

Shinkirō

Kawa akago

0   50   100   150
MILES

132   134   136   138

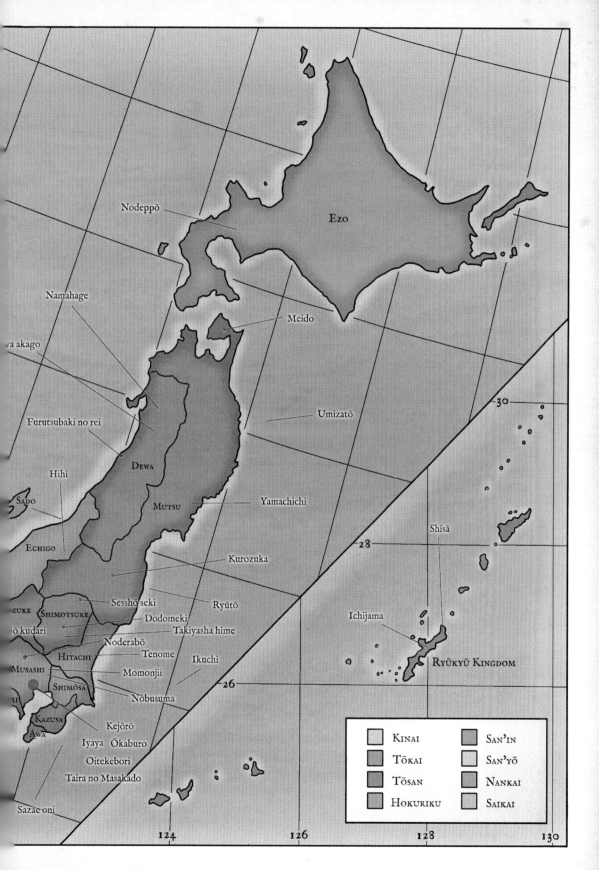

Nodeppō

Ezo

Namahage

Meido

ya akago

Furutsubaki no rei

Umizatō

Hihi

Dewa

30

Sado

Mutsu

Yamachichi

Echigo

Shīsā

Kurozuka

28

Sesshō'seki

Ryūtō

Ichijama

zuke

Shimotsuke

Dodomeki

ō kudari

Takiyasha hime

Noderabō

Tenome

Ikuchi

Hitachi

Musashi

Momonjii

Ryūkyū Kingdom

Shimōsa

Nobusuma

26

Kazusa

Kejōrō

Awa

Iyaya Ōkaburo

Oitekebori

Taira no Masakado

Sazae-oni

124   126   128   130

Kinai	San'in
Tōkai	San'yō
Tōsan	Nankai
Hokuriku	Saikai

Pronunciation Guide

The Japanese words in this book have been transliterated into English based on the Hepburn romanization rules. Care has been taken to write the Japanese names and words without altering their structure too much so that they are easy for English readers to digest.

Even with these considerations, figuring out the pronunciation of transliterated Japanese can sometimes be counterintuitive to native English speakers due to the vast differences between the two languages.

To help you read the Japanese words in this book, please follow this pronunciation guide.

Vowels

The five Japanese vowels are a, i, u, e, o, pronounced ah, ee, ooh, eh, and oh. As a rule, each vowel receives a full syllable, even when adjacent to another vowel. Avoid the temptation to blend vowels together. For example, the *ao* in ao bōzu should be read as two syllables, not one (ah-oh, not ow).

Macrons

Japanese occasionally uses the double vowels aa, uu, ee, oo, ou. In this book, double vowels are indicated with macrons to make them easier to read and pronounce: ā, ū, ē, ō. These macron vowels should be pronounced just like the vowels above and held for two syllables. For example, the *bōzu* in ao bōzu should be pronounced with three syllables, not two (boh-oh-zu, not boh-zu).

Compound Words

Japanese is written primarily with ideograms called kanji, and most words are only a few characters long. Compound words are fairly short in Japanese, and there is no hyphenation or other method to separate them as there is in English. This is not a problem when reading them in Japanese script, but when transliterating them into English it can lead to long, confusing strings of letters that are difficult to digest (for example, rokujōnomiyasundokoro, ushinokokumairi, and taizanfukunnosai).

To overcome this problem certain words and names have had spaces added to make them more legible and help with pronunciation. Broken apart this way, Rokujō no Miyasundokoro, ushi no koku mairi, and Taizan Fukun no Sai are comparatively easy to read and pronounce.

INTRODUCTION

WHAT ARE EVIL SPIRITS?

In Japan, it is said that there are 8 million *kami*. These spirits encompass every kind of supernatural creature; from malign to monstrous, demonic to divine, and everything in between. Most of them seem strange and scary—even evil—from a human perspective. They are known by myriad names: bakemono, chimimōryō, mamono, mononoke, obake, oni, and yōkai.

Yōkai is the most common catch-all term for the strange spirits of Japan. The word encompasses all of the supernatural creatures and phenomena which make up the spirit world. Within the realm of yōkai, there are a few significant categories. It is the nastiest of these spirits with which this book is concerned.

Oni (demons) stand apart from other yōkai due to their cultural and literary significance going back more than one thousand years. They are powerful and thoroughly evil spirits. Their sole occupation is to hurt humans and human civilization as much as possible. Long ago, oni was a generic term for all evil spirits, but it has evolved into a specific subset containing only the worst and most hellish of monsters. Oni play a prominent role in Japanese theater such as noh and kabuki, as well as other art forms. The female version of an oni is called a *kijo*.

Onryō (vengeful ghosts) hold a singular place in Japanese folklore and literature. These are ghosts of humans (and sometimes animals or yōkai) who return to haunt the world of the living. Though many kinds of ghosts exist, onryō are significant because of the sheer terror they inspired in the ancient aristocracy. Fear of their supernatural retribution—and efforts to appease these angry souls—has shaped the course of Japan's politics, history, and culture.

Kaibutsu (monsters) make up the broadest category of yōkai by far. This includes a number of subdivisions such as magical animals, *kaichō* (strange birds), *kaijū* (strange beasts), *tsukumogami* (artifact spirits), and transformed humans. Many of these yōkai were invented by Edo period bookmakers, looking to feed the insatiable appetite for ghost stories. Some of these monsters were once local kami who were long ago worshipped as gods. They were forgotten and devolved over time into amusing or scary versions of their former selves.

Kaii (strange phenomena) make up the final category. These includes *kaika* (strange fires) and *hi no tama* (fireballs), *tsukimono* (possession by spirits), enchantments, and other supernatural occurrences. Before modern medicine, mental illness was also included in this category. These phenomena can be caused by yōkai or black magic. Sometimes they occur for reasons unknown.

SORCERY AND THE MANIPULATION OF SPIRITS

Due to the prevalence of belief in evil spirits in ancient Japan, a number of traditions developed that attempted to tap the spirit world for human benefit. Most of these were syncretic, mixing Shinto, Buddhism, Confucianism, and Taoism beliefs and practices with local superstitions. As society developed, these traditions transformed into complex belief systems. Chief among them was the religion of yin and yang: Onmyōdō (陰陽道).

Onmyōdō is a Japanese occult philosophy and cult of magic that developed in the Heian period (794 to 1185 CE). Part natural science, part esoteric religion, Onmyōdō was a major political and social force for much of Japan's history.

Onmyōdō dealt primarily with divination and fortune telling, but covered a broad range of practices including: astrology and astronomy; the calendar and timekeeping; magic and medicine; driving evil spirits out of people, places, and things; creating protective wards against the supernatural; and subduing monsters. Practitioners of Onmyōdō were called onmyōji. They wielded considerable power for centuries.

Onmyōji were expected to use their occult knowledge on behalf of the state. They contacted the gods, buddhas, and kami to make official supplications. They prayed for the longevity of the emperor and protected officials against black magic and curses. Sometimes they used curses and magical spells against enemies.

Reading the future and making predictions was another important part of an onmyōji's job. The nobility of the Heian period based their lives around the predictions of onmyōji. Unlucky directions and inauspicious dates were avoided. If your house was located in an unlucky direction, you might not return home until a luckier date or direction was foretold. So strong was this belief that people canceled important meetings, turned down invitations, or remained absent from the imperial court based on the advice of an onmyōji.

The origins of Onmyōdō can be traced back to ancient China. Yin-yang philosophy and wuxing (the philosophy of five elements) were imported to Japan from the Tang Dynasty during the 6th century. They mixed together and combined with Japanese Shinto. Over the years, esoteric practices from Buddhism, Taosim, and Confucianism were added, along with the Chinese arts of astronomy, divination, fortune telling, calendar making, timekeeping, feng shui, and observational science. As its popularity among the nobility grew, more occult and esoteric elements were added.

For a few hundred years, onmyōdō was developed independently by onmyōji all over Japan. During the 10th century, two families—the Kamo clan and Abe clan—dominated the practice. With the establishment of the Onmyōryō (the imperial Bureau of Yin and Yang), the already immensely popular art became a centralized force under the control of the government.

But it did not last. Eventually, the political power of the onmyōji waned. The Onmyōryō was dismantled and shut down in 1869 after the Meiji Restoration. Onmyōdō came to be looked at as an ancient superstition, and lost its favor to new, forward-thinking, Western-inspired ideas. But the practices of onmyō magic did not vanish. They had been absorbed into other spiritual traditions and continued on under esoteric branches of Buddhism such as Shugendō and Kōshin.

MEETING EVIL SPIRITS

The existence of magic and the supernatural has always been an everyday fact of life in Japan. Sorcerers and priests are found even in the remotest parts of Japan, presiding over ceremonies, reading fortunes, asking the gods for blessings, and protecting people from the influences of evil spirits. Despite this protection, evil spirits remain a concern among people of all social strata. Superstitions set strict boundaries that cannot, and should not, be breached. Inauspicious days— such as the days when the night parade of one hundred demons roams the world—are marked on calendars. Certain activities are forbidden during those times.

Yōkai live in a world that parallels our own. Their lives resemble ours in many ways. They have societies and rivalries. They eat, sing, dance, play, fight, compete, and even wage war. Normally, we keep to our world and they keep to theirs. However, there are times and places where the boundaries between the worlds thin, and crossing over is possible:

There are borderlands where civilization ends and wild mountains begin, where rivers cut through the land, where the sea meets the shore. These are places where you might accidentally happen upon a spirit. In old Japan, leaving the safety of your village to go into the mountains was a dangerous task. Those who worked in the wilderness, like traders and woodcutters, had the most to fear. Yōkai roamed the untamed wilds.

The passage of time is also shrouded in occult mystery. The changing of the seasons is associated with the ebb and flow of yin and yang. Spirits appear more frequently during the solstices and equinoxes. During Obon, the summer festival honoring the dead, ancestral ghosts return from their world to spend time with the living. But the changing of the seasons and Obon are brief periods during each year—it is easy to take precautions during those times.

The cycle of night and day is the most constant—and unavoidable—reminder that evil spirits lurk everywhere. Humans thrive during the day, but during the night the supernatural takes over. Villagers whose work kept them out past sunset lived in fear of being abducted by mysterious creatures. *Ushi no koku*—the "hour of the ox"—is the Japanese equivalent of the witching hour. During this time—the period of deepest, darkest night between 1:00 and 3:00 am—even grass and trees are said to be asleep. Evil spirits are at their greatest power. People whose work keeps them away from their homes at this time are likely to run into danger, or be abducted by mysterious creatures.

There is only one time of day that is even more dangerous. The twilight hour—the border between daylight and darkness—is when the boundary between worlds is at its thinnest. Twilight is the easiest time for yōkai to cross into this world, or for humans to accidentally cross into theirs. Our world is still awake and active, but the world of the supernatural is beginning to stir. Superstition tells people to return to their villages and stay inside when the sun sets in order to avoid running into demons. This is why in Japanese the twilight hour is called *ōmagatoki*: "the hour of meeting evil spirits."

ŌMAGATOKI 逢魔時

TRANSLATION: the hour of meeting evil spirits

APPEARANCE: Ōmagatoki is the twilight hour between when the sun sets and the sky goes dark. It is not quite day, but not quite night. Shadows swallow everything. Your eyes start to play tricks on your mind. The border thins between *sekai*—the world we live in, belong to, and recognize—and *ikai*, the "other" world. Ikai is where the spirits live, a world about which we humans know next to nothing. During ōmagatoki, the evil spirits, the chimimōryō, wake up and move about freely. This is the hour when yōkai, yūrei, and other dark things cross over into our world.

The appearance of yōkai during ōmagatoki is said to be accompanied by a few telltale signs: a cold wind blowing; a strange smell in the air, like that of fish or blood; a sudden onset of darkness; a sudden chill that causes one's hairs standing on end.

INTERACTIONS: Humans and spirits normally have separate existences in different worlds. When those worlds come together, things become chaotic—particularly for humans. In order to avoid meeting the things that prowl the night, people would head home as the sun set and stay inside until morning. Woodcutters sleeping in mountain huts something heard the cutting down of trees at night, but found no evidence of it in the morning. Phantom waterfalls could be heard where there was no waterfall for miles around. Strange laughter and voices of inhuman things echoed throughout the forests. Children who wandered away from the village and got lost in the mountains could be spirited away by otherworldly things and taken to another world. Sometimes they would return years later, changed in some way.

ORIGIN: The first tales of encounters between humans and spirits came from woodsmen, travelers, criminals, and people whose livelihoods forced them away from the safety of their homes and villages at night. These men would return to their villages in the morning with stories of eerie experiences after twilight. Over time, these stories developed into the earliest superstitions, helping shape Japanese folklore, religion, and society into what they are today.

Ōmagatoki can be written two different ways: 逢魔時 literally means the hour of meeting evil spirits; 大禍時 literally means the hour of great calamity. Both of these readings illustrate the fear and apprehension that the ancient Japanese people felt towards the things that came at twilight.

CHIMI 魑魅

TRANSLATION: mountain spirit
ALTERNATE NAMES: sudama
HABITAT: mountains, forests, and other wilderness across Japan
DIET: varies, includes humans

APPEARANCE: Chimi have human-like faces and bestial bodies. They feed on the bodies of the dead—particularly the innards—and bring disease and evil things with them wherever they go. Chimi is both a specific and a general term for monsters that live in mountains, forests, swamps, stones, and other parts of nature.

INTERACTIONS: Chimi tend to be nasty, or at least mischievous. They trick humans who wander in the mountains, and cause them to lose their way. Once their prey is isolated, chimi attack, often killing their victims.

ORIGIN: The name chimi is derived from the ancient Chinese history known as *The Records of the Grand Historian*. Chi is the name of a tiger-like mountain god, while Mi is a swamp god with the head of a boar and the body of a human. Over time, the names of these gods combined into a term for all kinds of monstrously shaped nature spirits. In Japan, chimi are considered to be a kind of mountain kami.

Mōryō 魍魎

TRANSLATION: mountains, trees, streams, and rocks spirits
ALTERNATE NAMES: mizuha
HABITAT: streams, rivers, mountains, forests, graveyards, and wild areas all over Japan
DIET: human corpses

APPEARANCE: Mōryō are said to look like children about three years old, with red or black skin, red eyes, long ears, and long, beautiful hair. Like chimi, mōryō is both a specific yōkai and a general term for a large number of nature spirits that live in the wilderness. In general, mōryō refers to evil spirits which rob graves and eat corpses. In particular, while chimi refers to mountain and swamp spirits, mōryō refers to water spirits.

INTERACTIONS: The most defining feature of mōryō is that they feed upon the bodies of dead humans. They rob graves, dig corpses up out of the ground, and feast upon the rotting innards. They also interrupt funerals, using magic to distract the attendees so they can steal the corpses from their coffins while nobody is looking. Because of these behaviors, they are especially detested. Special methods have been even invented to prevent disturbances to the deceased.

Mōryō are afraid of oak trees and tigers. In ancient China it was common to plant oak trees in graveyards, and to adorn cemetery roads with stone tigers. Additionally, prior to interring a casket in the ground, a servant would enter the grave and prod around with a spear to make sure no mōryō were hiding in the ground. These practices did not catch on in Japan.

ORIGIN: Mōryō first appear in ancient Chinese records, where they were said to be minor nature spirits or demons. In Japan, they are considered to be water kami, and cooperate alongside chimi and other minor kami of the mountains. Many kinds of yōkai can be classified as mōryō, one of the most famous examples being the kappa. This leads to some confusion as to what this spirit's true nature is.

LEGENDS: In *Mimibukuro*—a collection of folktales collected during the Edo period—there is a story of a mōryō disguised as a human. Long ago there was a government official named Shibata. One evening, out of the blue, a servant informed Shibata that he would be leaving his service. When asked why, the servant replied that he was not actually a human, but a mōryō in disguise. His turn had come up to steal a corpse. The next day, he would have to travel to a nearby village and fulfill his duty as a mōryō. Sure enough, the servant vanished the following day. At the same time, dark clouds suddenly descended over a funeral service at the village the servant had mentioned. When the clouds cleared away, the corpse was missing from the coffin.

Chimimōryō 魑魅魍魎

Chimimōryō, combining the words chimi and mōryō, is a common term which refers to all evil spirits of the rivers and mountains. It's one of many catch-all terms for Japanese monsters, along with mononoke, bakemono, obake, minori, yōkai, and so on. Today, yōkai is the most common world used to refer to the vast menagerie of spirits in Japanese folklore. But in the past, each of these other terms has enjoyed varying levels of popularity.

JAMI 邪魅

TRANSLATION: wicked mountain spirit
HABITAT:
DIET: varies

APPEARANCE: Jami is not a clearly defined creature, but in general refers to manifestations of the ill will of the mountains and forests, awoken in order to do harm to humans. They are a subset of chimi, or mountain spirit—though they are much nastier.

INTERACTIONS: Jami are truly wicked and harmful towards people. Because there are so many different wicked spirits that can be considered to be jami, there isn't one particular ascribed behavior or danger. However, a common trait is that they are capable of possessing and inhabiting human bodies, infecting sickness and disease upon their human hosts.

ORIGIN: Along with chimi and mōryō, jami first appear in ancient Chinese histories describing the nature spirits that roam the land. As Chinese culture began to influence Japanese culture, scholars discovered these ancient books and incorporated their teachings into their own works. When these creatures were included in Japanese bestiaries and records, they became associated with various Japanese evil spirits.

LEGENDS: In the ancient Chinese hagiography *Biographies of Divine Transcendents*, a wise sage named Ōyō was able to cure sick people by drawing an image of a prison on the ground. He would then call the evil spirits out of the body of his patients. When the spirits came out, they would become trapped in the prison and the patient would be instantly cured of his sickness. The evil spirits trapped this way were said to be jami.

Shīsā シーサー

Translation: the Ryūkyūan pronunciation of *shishi* (lion-dogs)
Habitat: shrines, castles, graveyards, villages; often seen on rooftops
Diet: carnivorous

Appearance: Shīsā are small, lion-like yōkai which are found throughout the Ryūkyū islands. They are guardian deities which live in close proximity to humans. They are very similar to the lion-dogs found in other East Asian countries, but there are a few notable differences. Shīsā are native to the Ryūkyū archipelago, and are only found in Okinawa and the southern islands of Kyūshū. They are smaller and more dog-like than the lion-dogs found throughout the rest of Japan. In most of Japan, lion-dogs are found in pairs, yet the shīsā of Okinawa are often solitary.

Interactions: Shīsā are used as wards against evil spirits. They are most frequently found on the rooftops of houses and castles, or flanking village gates and gravesites. Shīsā are also commonly used as shrine and temple guardians. Shīsā found in male/female pairs show the influence from mainland Japan after the Ryūkyū islands were conquered. They represent the "*a*" and "*un*" syllables which make up the Sanskrit word *om*—the mystical sacred word found in Indian religions. The open-mouthed shīsā is usually the male, which beckons good luck and fortune. The close-mouthed shīsā is usually the female, which protects the village from natural disasters and evil spirits. However, their gender is a matter of controversy. In other depictions the open-mouthed shīsā is the female while the closed-mouthed shīsā is the male.

Origin: Shīsā are very close relatives of Japanese koma inu, and share the same ancestor: China's imperial guardian lions. However, while koma inu arrived in mainland Japan via Korea, shīsā were imported to the Ryūkyū islands directly from China, before they were a part of Japan. In fact, the name shīsā is actually the Ryūkyūan pronunciation of their Chinese name, shishi.

The Origin of Lion-dogs

Lion dogs are found in many East Asian countries. In China they are known as shishi, or stone lions. In Tibet they are known as ruishi, or snow lions. In Myanmar they are called chinthe. In Japan they are called koma inu, or Korean dogs. And in Ryūkyū they are called shīsā. Lions, however, are not found in any of these countries. The Asiatic lion is actually native to India.

The lion-dogs of Japan and Ryūkyū come from cultural diffusion due to heavy trade with the Tang dynasty of China. However, the usage of guardian lion statues goes back much further than the Tang Dynasty.

Lion imagery was first brought to China via trade along the Silk Road with Central Asian countries. In fact, the Chinese word for lion shares the same etymological root with the Persian word for lion. The usage of lions as symbols of protection and royalty in Central Asian art came via trade from India, where lion statues were frequently placed as guardians on both sides of statues of the Buddha. So the guardian lion-dogs we see throughout Japan actually have their origins in India.

The use of lions as symbols of protection goes back much further than the birth of Buddhism in India. Guardian lion statues can also be found Ancient Mesopotamia and Egyptian art, which was introduced to India and Central Asia from Greece during Alexander the Great's conquests. Perhaps shīsā are distantly related to the sphinx or lamassu...

HIYORIBŌ 日和坊

TRANSLATION: weather priest
ALTERNATE NAMES: teruteru bōzu
HABITAT: mountains (only appearing on sunny days)
DIET: unknown

APPEARANCE: Hiyoribō is a yōkai from Hitachi Province who looks like a stone priest. It blends in with its surroundings and is not easy to spot in its natural habitat.

BEHAVIOR: Hiyoribō calls forth the sun and creates good weather. It lives deep in the mountains, and can only be seen on sunny days. During rain or in bad weather, this yōkai remains hidden.

ORIGIN: Hiyoribō strongly resembles another weather yōkai from China known as the hiderigami. It may be that hiyoribō is simply another form of the hiderigami.

TERUTERU BŌZU

Hiyoribō is the origin of the traditional dolls called *teruteru bōzu*. Made of paper or cloth, teruteru bōzu look exactly like tissue-paper ghosts from Western countries, although their origins are unrelated. They became popular during the Edo period, when children would make them and pray to them for good weather the next day. If good weather came, eyes would be drawn on the teruteru bōzu, holy sake would be poured over them, and they would be washed away in a river.

HIDERIGAMI 魃

TRANSLATION: drought spirit
ALTERNATE NAMES: batsu, kanbo ("drought mother"), shinchi
HABITAT: mountains
DIET: atmospheric moisture

APPEARANCE: Hiderigami are grotesque, hairy humanoids which stand between two and three feet tall. They have a single eye on the top of their heads. They only have a single arm and a single leg, although they can run as fast as the wind. All hiderigami are female.

BEHAVIOR: Hiderigami are rarely encountered by humans. They live deep in the mountains and seldom travel out into human-inhabited lands. When they do, their presence can be felt over a wide area. A hiderigami's body exerts such an incredible heat that everywhere they go the ground dries up, clouds fail to form, and rain cannot fall. Not all water yields to the hiderigami's power—it is said that throwing a hiderigami into a toilet will kill it.

ORIGIN: Hiderigami originated in southern China, and come from a goddess. Their origin is recorded in some of the oldest Chinese records. When the legendary Yellow Emperor of China fought the warlord Chi You, he summoned a powerful goddess named Batsu to aid him in battle. Batsu contained a supernatural heat inside of her. When she released her power, the battle was quickly and decisively won in the emperor's favor. However, she had used so much of her power up that she was unable to return to heaven or contain her heat. While Batsu was nearby, waters dried up and rain would not fall. Her presence became a terrible problem for the emperor. Unable to kill her or to send her back to heaven, the emperor exiled the goddess to a far-away mountain and forbade her to return. Whether Batsu became the mother of the hiderigami or she became corrupted and transformed into this yōkai herself is unknown.

Ao bōzu 青坊主

TRANSLATION: blue monk
HABITAT: wheat and barley fields, uninhabited homes, lonely roads
DIET: varies from region to region; commonly children

APPEARANCE: Ao bōzu are generally depicted as large, one-eyed, blue-skinned priests with a strong connection to magic. However, local accounts vary greatly in details such as size, number of eyes, and habitat. In Okayama (old Bitchū, Bizen, and Mimasaka Provinces), they are described as two-eyed giants who take up residence in abandoned or uninhabited homes. In other stories, they appear in wheat fields, or on dark, lonely roads.

INTERACTIONS: In Shizuoka (old Tōtōmi, Suruga, and Izu Provinces), ao bōzu are said to appear in spring at sunset in wheat and barley fields. The transition from night to day is a popular theme in the tradition of onmyōdō. Further, the blue-green leaves of young barley have powerful connections to onmyō magic. Children who run and play through the fields in the evening might be snatched up and taken away by an ao bōzu. Thus, good children must go straight home after school and not tramp through the fields!

In Kagawa (old Sanuki Province), ao bōzu appear late at night to young women and ask them, "Would you like to hang by your neck?" If the woman says no, the ao bōzu disappears without a word. However, if she ignores him or says nothing, he attacks her with lightning speed. The ao bōzu knocks her out and hangs the poor woman by the neck.

In Yamaguchi (old Suō and Nagato Provinces), ao bōzu are considered minor deities. They appear before humans on the road and challenge them to sumo matches. Because Yamaguchi's ao bōzu are only as big as children, many have foolishly accepted the challenge. They quickly find themselves flung to the ground with god-like strength and potentially lethal speed.

ORIGIN: Very little is known about ao bōzu. Toriyama Sekien was the first to record them, and his illustration came without a single word of description other than their name. From their name we can glean a little bit of information; the word *ao* means blue or green, and can denote immaturity and inexperience. (Another well-known yōkai—ao nyōbō—uses this color in a similar manner.) As the original illustration was black-and-white, it may even be that this yōkai was never intended to be colored blue or green, but rather just as a mockery of what Toriyama Sekien saw as a corrupt and hypocritical priesthood. Nonetheless, due to their name, they are usually depicted in a sickly shade of blue or green.

The fact that ao bōzu have only one eye and are revered as minor gods in some places draws a strong parallel with another yōkai, the hitotsume kozō. Because of their similarity, there are theories suggesting a connection to the ancient spirit worship of old Japan. In this shamanistic proto-religion, one-eyed monsters were fallen mountain gods and bringers of evil, sent to do the bidding of larger deities. They could be kept at bay with woven baskets or other objects with many tiny holes. Monsters would view these as hundreds of eyes and flee, either out of fear or jealousy.

Because there are so many different accounts and so many different kinds of nasty priest yōkai, it's impossible to tell which, if any, describe the real ao bōzu.

FURUTSUBAKI NO REI 古椿の霊

TRANSLATION: old tsubaki spirit
HABITAT: tsubaki trees
DIET: sunlight, water, soil

APPEARANCE: In Japanese folklore, almost anything that lives long enough can develop a spirit and become a yōkai. When tsubaki trees (*Camellia japonica*, or the rose of winter) reach old age, their spirits gain the ability to separate from their host trees. They also manifest other strange and mysterious powers, which they use to bewitch and trick humans.

ORIGIN: The tsubaki is an evergreen tree with a peculiar trait. Instead of losing its flowers gradually, petal-by-petal, it drops them all at once to the ground. As a result, it has long been associated with death and strangeness in Japan. It is taboo to bring tsubaki flowers as gifts to hospitals or sick people.

LEGENDS: Long ago in Dewa Province, two merchants were walking along a mountain road when they passed a tsubaki tree. Suddenly, a beautiful young woman appeared on the road beside one of the merchants. She breathed on him, and he transformed into a bee. The young woman then disappeared into the tsubaki tree. The bee followed her and landed on a flower, however, the fragrance of the tree had turned into poison. As soon as the bee smelled it, the flower and the bee it dropped together to the ground. The remaining merchant picked up both the bee and the flower and rushed to a nearby temple. The priest recited prayers and read the sutras over the bee, but it sadly did not return to life or to its human form. Afterwards, the surviving merchant buried the bee and the flower together.

In Dewa Province, long ago, a man heard a sad and lonely voice coming from a tsubaki tree one night. A few days later, disaster befell the temple. This happened again and again, and soon the priests at the temple realized that the tsubaki would cry a warning every time something bad was about to happen. The tree was dubbed *Yonaki Tsubaki*, or "night-crying tsubaki," and still stands today in the temple Kanman-ji, where it has stood for over 700 years.

In Ōgaki, Gifu Prefecture (old Mino Province), there is an ancient burial mound. One year, historians excavated the burial mound and discovered some ancient artifacts, including a mirror and some bones. However, the man who discovered the artifacts died shortly after. The locals blamed it on a curse, and returned the artifacts to the mound. They planted a tsubaki on top of it. When the tsubaki grew old, it transformed into a yōkai tree. Since then, the glowing figure of a beautiful young woman has been seen by the roadside near the burial mound at night.

Ippondatara 一本踏鞴

Translation: one-legged bellows
Habitat: mountains
Diet: unknown, but kills humans one day per year

Appearance: Ippondatara has one thick, trunk-like leg and a single saucer-like eye. It lives deep in the mountains of Japan. It is especially well-known in the mountains bordering Wakayama and Nara Prefectures (old Kii and Yamato Provinces), though sightings have been reported in other neighboring prefectures as well.

Behavior: Ippondatara is a shy yōkai, and tends to stay away from inhabited areas. It moves about by hopping around and doing somersaults. It avoids humans, though on winter days it is not uncommon to find the unique prints of this yōkai's large, single foot in the snow.

Interactions: While it is mostly harmless, once per year on December 20th, the ippondatara turns violent. Those entering the mountains on that day who run into the ippondatara are squashed flat under its powerful foot. Because of this, December 20th is considered an unlucky day in the areas where this yōkai lives. People stay out of the mountains then.

Origin: The name ippondatara comes from *tatara*, the bellows that a blacksmith would use in the old days. This yōkai is said to resemble a master blacksmith who lost the use of one eye from years of starting at the intense flames, and lost the use of one leg from years of heavy work pumping the bellows.

There are many theories about the origin of this yōkai. In some villages, it is considered to be a cousin of a certain breed of kappa called gōrai which—every winter—transform from river spirits into mountain spirits called kashambo until they return to the rivers in spring. Ippondatara is said to be a kind of kashambo.

Other explanations describe the ippondatara as the ghost of a woodcutter who cut off one of his legs in penance for some crime. Or it may be the ghost of a famous one-legged, one-eyed robber named Hitotsudatara who lived in the mountains of Wakayama and had supernatural strength. It may even be the ghost of a giant boar who used to roam the mountains killing hunters. A high priest was able to bind the boar's spirit and keep it from harming people, but the conditions of the magic that binds this ghost allow it to roam free one day per year—on December 20th.

It has also been suggested that it is a kind of mountain kami which was corrupted over the ages and became a yōkai. A single eye is a common feature among mountain spirits, and other one-eyed yōkai (such as hitotsume kozō) originated as mountain kami as well.

OUNI 苧うに

TRANSLATION: ramie peat (named for her resemblance to these plants)
ALTERNATE NAMES: wauwau
HABITAT: deep in the mountains
DIET: omnivorous

APPEARANCE: Ouni looks like an ugly old woman with an angry face and a body covered in long, black hair. Ouni live deep in the mountains, away from civilization, and only occasionally appear before humans. They are a variety of yamauba, or mountain hag.

INTERACTIONS: Unlike most yamauba, ouni are friendly towards humans who treat them kindly. They occasionally visit rural houses or mountain huts late at night. When this happens, the ouni asks the owners of the house to give her free lodging and a meal for the night. If they are kind and invite her in, she spins an enormous amount of thread during the night for the family, and then she vanishes without a trace.

ORIGIN: Ouni's name comes from the Japanese words for ramie (*Boehmeria nivea*)—a fibrous plant that is used to make thread—and peat—the rotten muck found in swamps that comes from rotting plant matter. The first part of her name comes from the thread which she spins at night, usually in the form of ramie, as well as the long, black hair which covers her body and resembles thick threads. The second part refers to her filthy, black, hairy body, which makes her look like she is covered in dead vegetation.

Buruburu 震々

TRANSLATION: onomatopoeic; the sound of shivering
ALTERNATE NAMES: zozogami
HABITAT: human-inhabited areas
DIET: cowardice

APPEARANCE: Buruburu are invisible, but are usually depicted as shivering ghosts wearing tattered rags. The only way to know a buruburu is near is by recognizing the telltale signs: goose bumps and shivers.

INTERACTIONS: Buruburu are born when humans perform acts of cowardice, such as running away from battle. They possess people by clinging to their shirt collars and touching the backs of their necks. This causes their hair to stand on end and sends shivers down their bodies. Buruburu follow their victims and cause them to shudder in fear. They are sometimes referred to as the spirit of cowardice.

ORIGIN: The words *buruburu* and *zo* are Japanese onomatopoeia for the sound of shivering and the chill of fear. This spirit's name comes from the sound of the shivers that it causes to run down people's spines.

NAMAHAGE なまはげ

TRANSLATION: from a phrase meaning "peeled blisters"
ALTERNATE NAMES: amahage, amamehagi, namomihagi, appossha
HABITAT: mountainous regions in northern Japan
DIET: omnivorous

APPEARANCE: Namahage are a frightful demon-like yōkai which live in the mountains along the northern coast of the Sea of Japan. They look like oni, with bright red or blue skin, wild hair and eyes, large mouths full of sharp teeth, and often have horns sprouting from their forehead. They wear straw leggings and raincoats, and carry large blades.

INTERACTIONS: Once a year, during *koshōgatsu*—the first full moon of the New Year—the namahage descend from the mountains to scare villagers. They go from door to and brandish their knives, saying things like, "Any bad kids here?" They particularly enjoy scaring small children and new brides. Despite their ferocious appearance and behavior, they are actually well-meaning yōkai. They are sent down from the mountain as messengers of the gods to warn and chastise those who have been lazy or wicked.

ORIGIN: The name namahage comes from another taunt the namahage use: "Have your blisters peeled yet?" In the cold winter months, a lazy person who spent all of his or her time in front of the fireplace would get blisters from being too close to the heat for too long. *Namomi* is a regional name for these heat blisters, and *hagu* means to peel. The combination of those words became namahage.

Today, the namahage play a major part in New Year's festivities in Akita Prefecture (old Dewa Province). Villagers dress up in straw raincoats and leggings, don oni masks, and wield large knives. They go from house to house and play the part of namahage. Residents visited by these namahage give presents such as mochi to their "guests," while the namahage chastise kids and warn them to be good. Newlywed couples are also harassed by these namahage. They are expected to give an account of all of the evil deeds they did during their first year together, as well as serve sake and food to the namahage before sending them off.

While the name namahage is unique to Akita Prefecture, very similar yōkai are known by many different local names in neighboring regions: in Yamagata Prefecture they are known as amahage, in Ishikawa Prefecture they are known as amamehagi, and in Fukui Prefecture they are known as appossha.

Yamajijii 山爺

Translation: mountain geezer
Alternate names: yamanjii, yamachichi ("mountain father")
Habitat: deep in the mountains of Shikoku
Diet: omnivorous

Appearance: Yamajijii look like elderly men about 3-4 feet tall, with only one leg and one eye. In actuality, they have two eyes, but one of them is so huge and the other so tiny that they appear to have only one eye. Their bodies are covered in fine gray hair, and they can be found either wearing old clothes, tattered rags, or nothing at all. Their teeth are sharp and powerful—a yamajijii's bite is said to be strong enough to crush the bones of wild boars or monkeys.

Behavior: Yamajijii live in the mountains far from human settlements. They rarely appear before humans, but their tracks are easily recognizable. They leave deep, sunken footprints about 12 inches long every 6 to 7 feet (from hopping about on one leg). Because their bite is so strong, hunters would sometimes tame yamajijii and use them to drive away wolves. They also have the uncanny ability to read peoples' thoughts. They are most well-known, however, for their powerful voices. The cry of a yamajijii is so powerful it blows the leaves off of branches, splits trees and moves rocks, reverberates through the mountains, and shakes the heavens and the earth. They enjoy shouting contests, and will occasionally allow a human to challenge them. However, humans who are close to a yamajijii when it shouts sometimes have their eardrums burst, or even die.

Legends: An old story tells of a brave hunter who challenged a yamajijii to a shouting contest. On the hunter's turn, he fired his rifle when he shouted, winning the contest. Later, the yamajijii realized he had been tricked. He shape-shifted into a spider and snuck into the hunter's bed to attack him in his sleep. In some versions of the tale, the clever hunter prepared for the shouting contest by praying to the gods of Ise and crafting a holy bullet inscribed with their names. This bullet had a special power: when fired it would never miss. Because of its magic, whenever the hunter carried it with him it would invariably attract the attention of yōkai. However, any time a yamajijii came near enough to threaten him, the hunter would display the bullet, and the yamajijii would flee in terror.

A tale from Awa Province tells of a group of woodcutters warming themselves by a fire in a cabin when yamajijii suddenly appeared. The terrified woodcutters all had the same idea—kill the yōkai! The yamajijii read their minds one by one. Suddenly, one of the logs in the fire split with a loud snap! The yamajijii thought there must be a mind he could not read among the hunters. He fled the cabin in terror.

A legend from Tosa Province tells of a kind yamajijii who gave a sorghum seed to a poor farmer as a gift. The farmer sowed the seed and that year was blessed with an incredible harvest. That winter, the yamajijii returned and asked for some mochi to eat. The grateful farmer gladly gave the yamajijii as much mochi as it could eat. The next year another great harvest followed, and again the yamajijii came back in the winter to ask for mochi. Each year, the yamajijii was able to eat more and more mochi, until it was able to eat three huge barrels-full. The farmer became afraid of losing his fortune, and they next time it came he gave the yamajijii a pile of burned stones, passing them off as yakimochi—baked rice cakes. The yamajijii ate them, but soon began to feel sick and hot. The farmer offered a cup of hot oil, passing it off as tea, but the yamajijii realized the farmer's trick. Surprised and hurt, it fled into the woods, but died before it could get back to its home. Afterwards, the farmer's family fell into ruin and was never rich again.

SANSEI 山精

TRANSLATION: mountain sprite
ALTERNATE NAMES: sanki ("mountain demon")
HABITAT: mountains
DIET: crabs and frogs

APPEARANCE: Sansei are small humanoid spirits that live deep in the mountains. They range in size from about one foot tall to three or four feet tall. Their most noticeable trait is their single leg, which is turned around backwards. They are known as the leaders of all animals which live in the mountains. Their diet mainly consists of frogs and stone crabs, which they are particularly fond of broiling with salt.

INTERACTIONS: Sansei occasionally sneak into woodcutters' houses and mountain huts to steal salt, which they use to flavor the crabs. Though not very aggressive, they sometimes attack humans. When this happens, if one calls out, "Hiderigami!" the sansei will flee in terror. However, if one calls out, "Sansei!" instead, that person will meet some horrible fate, such as falling ill or having their house catch on fire.

SATORI 覚

TRANSLATION: enlightenment
ALTERNATE NAMES: kaku, yamako, kuronbō
HABITAT: deep in the mountains of central Japan
DIET: carnivorous; occasionally humans

APPEARANCE: Satori are strange, intelligent ape-men found in the Japanese Alps. They are roughly man-sized, and appear similar to larger versions of the native monkeys found in the region.

INTERACTIONS: Satori appear to travelers on mountain roads, or to folks living in mountain huts far from civilization. If the opportunity presents itself, they gladly dine on anyone they can get their hands on. In cases where they encounter a lone human female, they often take her away into the mountains and rape her. Satori are most well known for their uncanny ability to read people's minds and then speak their thoughts faster than the individuals can get the words out themselves. This makes it difficult to hunt, trick, or escape from a hungry satori. The one thing they fear is the unexpected. Should something unforeseen happen, such as being hit by an unseen object, satori grow frightened and run away. One of the only ways to avoid being eaten by these yōkai is to completely empty your mind. With no mind to read, the satori grows bored and wanders away.

ORIGIN: The word *satori* literally means "enlightenment," in the Buddhist sense. The satori, with its uncanny ability to read thoughts, comes across as a kind of enlightened being to scared travelers, which is how it got its name. This also relates to the method of escaping a satori—true enlightenment comes from emptying one's mind of distracting, worldly thoughts, just as salvation from the hungry satori comes from an empty, zen-like mindset.

The origin of the satori is not entirely clear. Edo-period encyclopedias relate satori with *yamako*, apes from western China that capture women to rape or eat. It has also been theorized that satori are cousins of the yamabiko, a small, monkey-like yōkai. The satori's ability to read people's minds and the yamabiko's ability to mimic their words are rooted in the same folklore. More recent folklorists have suggested that satori are fallen mountain gods of the ancient proto-Shinto religion which were corrupted into yōkai over the ages.

IMORI 守宮

TRANSLATION: gecko

APPEARANCE: Imori are the ghosts of dead warriors transformed into geckos. They haunt the forgotten, overgrown ruins where they lost their lives, attacking and harassing trespassers.

ORIGIN: This yōkai's name is somewhat confusing—it is written with the kanji for gecko, which is normally pronounced *yamori*; yet in this case the name is pronounced *imori*, which means newt. When written it implies that this is a gecko yōkai, but when spoken it sounds like a newt yōkai—in actuality it refers to a gecko yōkai.

LEGENDS: Long ago in in Echizen Province there was a monk named Jingai Shuso. He lived as a hermit out in the mountains. He subsisted off of wild mountain plants and whatever charity the people from the local village would bring him. He spent almost all of his time in secluded meditation. One day Jingai was reading near the ruins of Yu no O castle, when suddenly a tiny man appeared and started talking to him. The man was only about 5 or 6 inches tall and wore a black hat and carried a cane. Being a good monk, Jingai did not let the stranger interrupt his studies. He continued reading. This angered the little man. He scolded Jingai, but Jingai still paid no attention. The tiny man became angry. He hopped up on to his cane and flew at Jingai. Jingai brushed him away with his fan, and the tiny man fell to the ground. He swore to get revenge on Jingai.

Shortly afterwards, five women, about 5 or 6 inches tall, came up to Jingai and scolded him. Suddenly, there were 10,000 of these tiny people, with sleeves rolled up and armed with canes. They swarmed upon Jingai and began to beat him with their canes. In the distance, Jingai saw their general—a tiny warrior in red lacquered armor. The general called out, "Get out of here and never return, or else we will pop your eyes and slice off your ears and nose!" Some of the tiny men had climbed upon Jingai's shoulders and began to eat his ears and nose. Jingai knocked them off and ran away.

Jingai ran to a ruined gatehouse. When he arrived, there were thousands of tiny men swarming over it. They knocked Jingai down, and another general said to him, "You were rude to our friends! We will cut off your hands and feet!" Thousands of tiny katanas were drawn from their tiny sheaths. Jingai was surrounded.

Terrified, Jingai apologized for not considering their feelings. He begged them to spare him. The general told him that if Jingai was truly sorry, he could go. The general ordered his men to eject the monk from the gatehouse, and Jingai ran away.

The next day, Jingai investigated castle ruins. He discovered a large hole in the ground that was swarming with geckos. Gathering some local villagers for help, he dug up the hole. It was over 3 meters deep, and filled with over 20,000 geckos! Deep inside, he discovered a 12 inch long gecko, which he realized must have been the general. The village elders explained that long ago an ally of Nitta Yoshisada built a castle near there, and it was destroyed in a battle. The souls of the dead warriors and the lord haunted the remains of the old castle well. Ever since, they had been causing all kinds of mischief in the area.

Jingai began chanting sutras. By the time he finished chanting, the thousands of geckos were dead. Jingai took pity upon the poor beasts. He and the villagers collected the bodies, burnt them on a funeral pyre, and buried them. On top of the mountain of ashes they built a proper grave for the fallen warriors.

Tsurubebi 釣瓶火

Translation: well bucket fire
Alternate names: tsurube otoshi, tsurube oroshi
Habitat: coniferous trees deep in the forests of Shikoku and Kyūshū
Diet: none

Appearance: Tsurubebi are small tree spirits which appear at night, deep in coniferous forests. They take the form of bluish-white orbs of fire which bob up and down in the branches. Occasionally they drop to the forest floor and float back up into the trees. Their name comes from the way they bob about in the trees, which resembles a well bucket swinging back and forth. Sometimes the vague shape of a human or bestial face can be seen in the flames.

Behavior: Tsurubebi do very little other than bob up and down or drop from branches. Their flames produce no heat and do not burn the trees that they live in. Nor do these yōkai pose any other known threat. While tsurubebi are most often considered to be tree spirits, it has also been suggested that they are closely related to another yōkai named tsurube otoshi. These two yōkai share many similarities, including their names, coniferous habitat, and dropping-down behavior. However, while tsurube otoshi are malevolent and dangerous, tsurubebi appear to be entirely benign and uninterested in humans.

Furaribi ふらり火

TRANSLATION: aimless fire
ALTERNATE NAMES: buraribi, sayuribi
HABITAT: riverbanks
DIET: none

APPEARANCE: Furaribi are small, flying creatures wreathed in flames. They have the bodies of birds, and their faces are somewhat dog-like. Furaribi appear late at night near riverbanks. They are a type of hi no tama, or fireball yōkai. They do very little except for float about aimlessly, which is how they got their name.

ORIGIN: Furaribi are created from the remains of souls which have not properly passed on to the next life. This is most often due to not receiving proper ceremonial services after dying. In Japan there are a number of important ceremonies performed at fixed intervals which occur for many years after someone's death—missing even one of these could cause a soul to become lost and unable to rest. Furaribi are one example of such lost souls.

LEGENDS: In the late 16th century, Etchū Province was ruled by a samurai named Sassa Narimasa. Narimasa kept a very beautiful concubine named Sayuri in his household. Sayuri was not well liked by the female servants or other women in Narimasa's household. They were jealous of her beauty and of Narimasa's love for her. One day, these women conspired against Sayuri and started a rumor that she had been unfaithful to Narimasa with one of his own men. Narimasa flew in a fit of jealous rage, murdered Sayuri, and took her body down to the Jinzū River. He hung her corpse from a tree and carved it into pieces with his sword. Next, he captured Sayuri's entire extended family—18 people in all—and executed them in the same manner. Afterwards, their tortured souls aimlessly wandered the riverbanks every night as furaribi.

It is said if you go down to the riverside and call out, "Sayuri, Sayuri!" late at night, the floating, severed head of a woman will appear, pulling and tearing at her hair in a vengeful fury. As for Sassa Narimasa, he was later defeated by Toyotomi Hideyoshi. Some have attributed his defeat by Hideyoshi to the vengeful curse of Sayuri's ghost.

UBAGABI 姥ヶ火

TRANSLATION: old hag fire
HABITAT: riverbanks

APPEARANCE: Ubagabi are a kind of hi no tama, or fireball yōkai. They appear on rainy nights near riverbanks, and take the form of 1-foot diameter balls of flame with the faces of old women in them. They can also appear as chickens, but do not remain in this form for long. They are created out of the ghosts of old women who were caught stealing oil and died of shame.

BEHAVIOR: Ubagabi have the uncanny ability to fly long distances in the blink of an eye—up to 4 kilometers. Occasionally, they graze a person's shoulder and then continue off into the darkness. The unfortunate people whom they bounce off of invariably end up dying within three years. However, if they are quick enough and shout, "*Abura sashi!*" (oil thief) just as an ubagabi comes flying towards them, the yōkai will vanish. The shame at being called out as an oil thief is too much to bear even in death.

LEGENDS: Long ago in Kawachi Province there lived an old woman who was very poor. In order to make ends meet, she stole oil from the lamps at Hiraoka Shrine—a terrible crime in an age when oil was rare and precious. Eventually she was caught by the shrine's priests and her crime was exposed. From then on, the people of her village shunned her, and would shout out at her, calling her an oil thief. So great was the old woman's shame that she went to the pond behind the shrine and committed suicide. Such unclean deaths never turn out well. Instead of dying properly she turned into a yōkai. To this day, the pond behind Hiraoka Shrine is known by locals as *Ubagabi Ike* ("the pond of the ubagabi").

Sagari さがり

TRANSLATION: hanging
HABITAT: hackberry trees
DIET: none

APPEARANCE: Sagari are strange apparitions from western Japan and Kyūshū, particularly Okayama and Kumamoto Prefectures (old Higo, Bitchū, Bizen, and Mimasaka Provinces). They take the form of grotesque horse heads, which drop down from hackberry trees to startle travelers on the road.

BEHAVIOR: Sagari don't do very much other than drop down right in front of your face and scream their unholy cry. However, those who hear a sagari's whinnying and screaming may be stricken with a terrible fever.

ORIGIN: Sagari come from the spirits of horses which die on the road and are discarded and left to rot where they fall. The horses' souls get caught in the trees as they rise from the bodies. The ones that stick in the trees cannot pass on to the next word and transform into these yōkai.

Yosuzume 夜雀

Translation: night sparrow
Alternate names: tamoto suzume, okuri suzume
Habitat: remote mountain passes and roads
Diet: seeds and insects

Appearance: The yosuzume is a rare bird yōkai found on the island of Shikoku and in neighboring areas. As their name suggests, they are nocturnal, appearing on remote mountain passes and forested roads late at night. Like ordinary sparrows, they are noisy birds usually found in large flocks.

Interactions: Yosuzume appear to travelers at night, swirling around them in a creepy, unnatural swarm. By themselves they don't do any particular harm other than startling people; however they are a sign of bad luck and bring terrible evil to those whom they surround. Because of this, locals have superstitious chants to say at night to keep yosuzume away. Roughly translated, one of them goes: *"Chi, chi, chi calls the bird | maybe it wants a branch | if it does, hit it with one."* Another one goes, *"Chi, chi, chi calls the bird | please blow soon | divine wind of Ise."*

In some places, yosuzume are known as tamoto suzume, or "sleeve sparrows." Their appearance was a sign that wolves, wild dogs, or other yōkai were nearby. Their call is mysteriously only ever heard by a single individual, even when traveling in groups. It was considered bad luck if a tamoto suzume jumped into your sleeve while walking, and so travelers held their sleeves tightly shut when traveling in areas inhabited by these birds.

In other areas, yosuzume are not seen as bad omens; they are instead warning signs that a more dangerous yōkai, the okuri inu, is nearby. For this reason, the yosuzume is also known as the okuri suzume, or "sending sparrow." Its call is said to be a reminder to travelers to watch their footing on the dangerous mountain paths.

Okuri inu 送り犬

TRANSLATION: sending-off dog
ALTERNATE NAMES: okuri ōkami (sending-off wolf)
HABITAT: dark mountain passes, forested roads
DIET: carnivorous; particularly fond of humans

APPEARANCE: Okuri inu are nocturnal dog- or wolf-like yōkai which haunt mountain passes, forested roads, and similar locations. They resemble ordinary dogs and wolves in all but their ferocity; they are much more dangerous than their mortal counterparts.

BEHAVIOR: Okuri inu follow lone travelers late on the road at night. They stalk their prey, keeping a safe distance, but following footstep for footstep. You are safe so long as you keep walking. If you should trip or stumble, the okuri inu will pounce and rip you to shreds. The "sending-off" part of its name comes from how it follows closely behind travelers, trailing behind them as if it were a friend sending them off on their way.

Okuri inu are somewhat of a blessing and a curse. On the one hand, if you should trip and fall, it will pounce with supernatural speed and gobble you up. On the other hand, they are so ferocious that while they are following someone, no other dangerous yōkai or wild animals will come near. As long as you keep your footing, you are safe. But traveling in the dark over root-infested, rocky mountain footpaths does not make for easy footing—especially for merchants carrying large packs of whatever it is they are going to sell!

INTERACTIONS: The okuri inu has a special relationship with another yōkai, the yosuzume. This eerie bird's nocturnal song is often a warning that an okuri inu is following you. If you hear the yosuzume's "chi, chi, chi" song, it is a sign to take extra care to watch your footing so that the okuri inu doesn't have you for dinner that night.

In the unfortunate case that you should stumble on the road, there is one chance for survival: if you fake it so it looks like you did it on purpose, the okuri inu will be tricked into thinking you were just taking a short rest, and it won't pursue. You do this by saying "*Dokkoisho!*" ("Heave-ho!") or "*Shindoi wa!*" ("This is exhausting!") and quickly fixing yourself into a sitting position. Sigh, sit for a bit, and then continue on your way. The okuri inu will wait patiently for you.

If you should make it out of the mountains safely, turn around and call out, "Thanks for seeing me off!" Afterwards, that okuri inu will never follow you again. Further, when you get home, wash your feet and leave out a dish of something for the okuri inu. This shows your gratitude to the okuri inu for watching over you.

ORIGIN: Superstitions related to the okuri-inu are extremely old, and found in all parts of Japan. Wolves and wild dogs have existed on the Japanese isles for as long as humans have, and the legend of the okuri inu originated in the mists of pre-history.

In modern Japanese, the word okuri ōkami also applies to predatory men who go after young women, pretending to be sweet and helpful but with ulterior motives. That word comes from this yōkai.

In Izu and Saitama, there is a similar yōkai known as the okuri itachi. This is a weasel that works in roughly the same way as the okuri inu; only if you take off one of your shoes and throw it at it, the weasel will eat the shoe, run away, and leave you in peace.

Hihi 比々

TRANSLATION: none; based on the Chinese name for the same creature
HABITAT: deep in the mountains
DIET: carnivorous

APPEARANCE: Hihi are large, monkey-like beasts which live deep in the mountains. They have long, black hair and wide mouths with long, flapping lips. Old legends say when a monkey reaches a very old age it will transform into a hihi.

BEHAVIOR: Hihi are fast runners and primarily feed on wild animals such as boars. They batter them down and snatch them up just as a bird of prey snatches up small animals. The hihi gets its name from the sound of its laugh. When it sees a human it can't help but burst into laughter, letting out a loud, "*Hihihihi!*" When it laughs, its long lips curl upwards and completely cover its eyes.

INTERACTIONS: While hihi feed primarily on wild beasts, they will also prey on humans given the opportunity. They are known to catch and run off with human women in particular. If a hihi grabs a human there is only one way to escape—by making it laugh. While it is laughing it is blinded by its own lips. It can be taken down by striking it in the middle of the forehead with a sharp spike.

Hihi are sometimes confused with other mountain-dwelling, monkey-like yōkai, such as yamawaro and satori. The hihi are much bigger, more violent, and far more dangerous. Some stories say that, like satori, hihi have the ability to speak human words and read human hearts and thoughts. They are valued for their blood, which is a vivid, bright red. If used as a dye, the bright red color will never fade or run. If drunk, the imbiber gains the ability to see invisible demons and spirits.

ORIGIN: The origin of the hihi lies in ancient Chinese mythology, where they were believed to be supernatural monkeys that lived in the mountains. These legends were brought over to Japan by folklorists during the Middle Ages. In modern Japanese, hihi is the word for baboon, which takes its name from its resemblance to this yōkai.

NOBUSUMA 野衾

TRANSLATION: wild quilt
ALTERNATE NAMES: tobikura (flying warehouse)
HABITAT: forests and mountains
DIET: primarily blood; also fire, nuts, fruit and berries

APPEARANCE: Bats which live to a very old age develops magical powers and change into nobusuma. They look almost identical to *musasabi*, or Japanese giant flying squirrels—although nobusuma are much more dangerous.

BEHAVIOR: Nobusuma eat nuts, fruit, and berries like other animals, but they also feed on fire and by sucking blood from humans and small animals such as cats. They attack travelers walking the roads at night. Nobusuma swoop down from the trees onto the faces of their unsuspecting victims. They latch on and begin sucking blood. When they do not need to feed, they simply swoop down and blow out lanterns and torches. Then they fly back into the night sky with a creepy cry of "gaa gaa!"

ORIGIN: While nobusuma are born from long-lived bats, the transformation does not stop there. They have several evolutions. Once a nobusuma reaches old age, it transforms again, either into a yamachichi or a momonjii.

This yōkai should not be confused with the nobusuma (野襖) from Tosa Province, whose name is pronounced the same but uses different kanji. That nobusuma is actually a variety of a different yōkai called nurikabe.

YAMACHICHI 山地乳

TRANSLATION: none; just the name for this monster
ALTERNATE NAMES: yamajiji, satorikai
HABITAT: deep in secluded mountains
DIET: life force (in the form of the breath of sleeping humans)

APPEARANCE: Yamachichi live in northeastern Japan and originally come from bats. A long-lived bat transforms into a nobusuma, which then transforms into a yamachichi after many more years. These yōkai resemble monkeys with pointed mouths and sucking lips.

BEHAVIOR: Yamachichi live deep in the mountains and pay visits to houses late at night. They steal the breath from sleeping human victims, sucking it out of their mouths with their pointed lips. After sucking away all of their victims' sleeping breath, yamachichi tap their victims on the chest, and then flee into the night. Humans who have had their breath stolen this way will die the next day. However, if a yamachichi should be caught in the act of stealing breath—either by the victim or by another witness—it will flee. Its victim will have their life span greatly increased instead.

ORIGIN: The name yamachichi only appears in the *Ehon Hyakumonogatari*, an Edo period yōkai bestiary. Thus, very little is known about them. The characters used to write the name literally mean "mountainous region" and "breast" or "milk." These are most likely *ateji*—characters assigned phonetically without regard to the original meaning of the word. The original meaning of the name is mysterious and the only explanation given is that they are called yamachichi because they live hidden away in the mountains.

Because they are similar in shape to satori, yamachichi are often confused with that yōkai. Yamachichi have picked up the alternative name satorikai.

Momonjii 百々爺

TRANSLATION: hundred hundred (i.e. really old) geezer
HABITAT: dark roads and mountain passes
DIET: omnivorous

APPEARANCE: Momonjii derive from long-lived nobusuma, which originally come from long-lived bats. They are mysterious yōkai that take the form of hairy, bestial old men who wander the wilds and assault passersby—particularly crying or misbehaving children. Momonjii appear late at night on the road, when the wind blows strongly. Those who are unfortunate enough to meet them suddenly fall sick.

ORIGIN: The name momonjii was created by a complicated combination of Japanese puns and wordplay. It is formed from the words *momonga* and *gagoji*.

Momonga is the Japanese word for a small flying squirrel—but long ago the momonga and musasabi (the Japanese giant flying squirrel) were thought to be the same animal. Their names were used interchangeably. The yōkai nobusuma (from which momonjii evolve) closely resemble musasabi; so the name momonga was used interchangeably to refer to nobusuma.

Gagoji is a regional word for a bogeyman-like monster who assaults children. The name is a regional variation of the famous demon Gagoze of Gangō-ji. Momonga and gagoji were combined to form momonjii—a scary, child-assaulting monster related to the nobusuma.

During the Edo period, there was a strict prohibition on eating meat from certain animals such as deer and boar. These forbidden animals were collectively referred to as momonjii. To get around this prohibition, shops began selling animal meat as "medicine" instead of food. These "medicine" shops were called *momonjiya*, and the meat sold there was believed to ward off disease. The fact that this yōkai resembles a wild animal and also brings disease is an cynical reference to momonjii and momonjiya.

The "medicine" sold at momonjiya was given nicknames in order to disguise its true contents. Deer meat was called *momiji*, or maple leaves, and boar meat was called *botan*, or peony. This secret imagery persists in things like hanafuda playing cards which show deer with maple leaves and boar with peonies. Toriyama Sekien was aware of the imagery in hanafuda cards; when he first illustrated the momonjii he drew it hiding in a pile of maple leaves and created yet another connected between this yōkai and the prohibition of wild animal meat.

Nodeppō 野鉄砲

TRANSLATION: wild gun
HABITAT: mountains and forests
DIET: blood

APPEARANCE: Nodeppō are animal yōkai which live in northern Japan, deep in forested mountain valleys. Nodeppō resemble flying squirrels, but are actually born from animals called *mami*, which resemble badgers. When mami reach old age, they transform into nodeppō.

BEHAVIOR: Nodeppō closely resemble nobusuma in appearance and behavior. They swoop down from trees at night and extinguish flames. They latch on to humans' faces, smothering them and sucking out their blood. In fact, in some places nodeppō and nobusuma are thought to be the same creature.

While both nodeppō and nobusuma smother people's faces and blind them with their webbed arms and legs, nodeppō can do something unique amongst yōkai: it shoots bats out of its mouth like bullets from a gun. The nodeppō is able to spit a stream of bats out of its mouth towards the faces of its victims, blinding them in a cloud of angry bats. This distinguishing feature also gives the nodeppō its name.

MUJINA AND MAMI AND TANUKI, OH MY!

Mami has been used to describe a number of creatures across Japan. In olden times, depending on where you lived, mami could refer to some or all of the following: tanuki (raccoon dogs), musasabi (Japanese giant flying squirrels), momonga (flying squirrels), mujina (badgers), or anaguma (another word for badgers). To further add to the confusion, in some regions the kanji for these animals might be switched. As you traveled from region to region, the meaning of written words would change too. Often times these animals were considered to be the same animal. They were seen as different stages in the life of one creature, in the same way a caterpillar becomes a butterfly or a tadpole becomes a frog.

Noderabō 野寺坊

TRANSLATION: wild temple priest
HABITAT: abandoned, ruined temples
DIET: sadness

APPEARANCE: Noderabō appear as forlorn, grotesque priests dressed in tattered rags. They appear late at night in abandoned, overgrown, ruined temples, and haunt the temple grounds. They occasionally ring the large temple bells.

ORIGIN: Noderabō are the ghosts of priests who committed some kind of sin and died in dishonor. Most often they are those who fell to vices forbidden to the clergy, such as attachment to women or money. No longer welcome in towns and cities, they flee to abandoned temple ruins located out in depressed rural areas. Eventually, they transform into yōkai.

LEGENDS: In Saitama Prefecture there is a place called Nodera which gets its name from this yōkai. Long ago in Musashi Province, a prankster decided to steal the large bronze bell from the town's temple. However, he was spotted in the act by one of the local townspeople and fled. He dropped the bell into a pond, where it got stuck. It was too heavy and dangerous to remove, so the townspeople decided just to leave it in the pond. Eventually the pond became known as *Kanegaike* ("Bell Pond").

One day, a lazy priest boy was given a job by the high priest of the temple. Instead of doing what he was bid, the boy spent the day playing with other neighborhood children. When it came time for him to face the high priest, he was so ashamed that he became depressed and drowned himself in Kanegaike. After that, the villagers could hear the sound of crying every night echoing off of the great bronze bell, coming from deep within Kanegaike pond. The priest boy became known as the ghost of Nodera, or the noderabō.

71

FURUUTSUBO 古空穂

TRANSLATION: old quiver

APPEARANCE: Furuutsubo are the beloved quivers of slain archers who died particularly tragic deaths. These quivers—along with other arms and armor—develop life force due to the residual energies left behind by their owners. They begin to move around on their own.

Legend: The most famous furuutsubo was the quiver which belonged to Miura Yoshiaki, a military commander who lived at the end of the Heian period. Yoshiaki was a brave warrior, skilled in sword and bow. For the Genpei War, he fought on the side of the Minamoto clan. As the enemy was bearing down during a terrible siege, Yoshiaki arranged for his household to escape from the castle. Then, as the last few survivors made it out safely, he remained alone. Yoshiaki stayed behind to defend the castle against the invading army. He sacrificed his life. After his heroic death, his favorite quiver was heartbroken at the loss of its master. It took on a life of its own and became this yōkai.

ABUMIGUCHI 鐙口

TRANSLATION: stirrup mouth

APPEARANCE: Abumiguchi were once stirrups belonging to a warrior who fell in battle. The stirrups were left on the battlefield, forgotten. Upset at losing their purpose, a soldier's implements can transform into tsukumogami. Like faithful hounds, abumiguchi wait in the fields for their masters, who will sadly never return.

KURA YARŌ 鞍野郎

TRANSLATION: saddle rascal

APPEARANCE: Kura yarō are saddles whose masters have been slain. They take on lives of their own and act like warriors.

LEGENDS: The most famous kura yarō was once the saddle of Kamata Masakiyo, the first and foremost retainer to Minamoto no Yoshitomo, general and head of the Minamoto clan. After losing a battle during the Heiji Rebellion (1160 CE), he and his lord fled from Kyōto. But they were betrayed and murdered by an ally. Kamata Masakiyo's wrath at being betrayed remained after his death and became attached to his saddle, which transformed into a tsukumogami. Afterwards, his saddle would pick up sticks and prance about like a warrior, fighting everything it could. Even after his death, Masakiyo's weapons were a loyal to his cause.

KOSENJŌBI 古戦場火

TRANSLATION: ancient battlefield fire
ALTERNATE NAMES: kosenjō no hi
HABITAT: ancient battlefields
DIET: none

APPEARANCE: Kosenjōbi are a type of onibi, or demon fire. They gather in places were bloody battles have been fought. Kosenjōbi appear as countless orbs of flame which float about aimlessly through the air.

BEHAVIOR: Kosenjōbi are formed from the blood of the countless warriors and animals which died in battle and never passed on to Nirvana. The blood soaks into the earth and rises up into the air at night. It creates fiery shapes. Kosenjōbi occasionally take on the form of wounded warriors and animals. These phantoms search for their missing body parts or just wander forlornly across the battlefield.

Though eerie to look at, kosenjōbi do not harm the living.

KAWA AKAGO 川赤子

TRANSLATION: river baby
ALTERNATE NAMES: kawa akaji
HABITAT: rivers, streams, ponds, swamps
DIET: omnivorous

APPEARANCE: Kawa akago are cousins of the kappa, and trickster yōkai. They look like small, red-skinned babies.

INTERACTIONS: Kawa akago appear on riverbanks and call out to passersby, perfectly mimicking the sound of crying human babies: "Waah! Waah!" (Japanese: "*Ogyaa! Ogyaa!*") When someone wanders down to the river's edge, the kawa akago retreats further into the underbrush and calls out again. This continues with the yōkai leading its victim further and further into the river. Finally, it sneaks up under the unsuspecting human, pulls his legs out from under him, and sends him tumbling into the river. While this is only meant as a prank, some people drown in this manner. This makes kawa akago a fairly dangerous yōkai.

ORIGIN: Similar yōkai called yama akago (mountain baby) are found in Akita Prefecture (old Dewa Province). They hide in leaf piles in the mountains, and when people step on the leaves, they call out in a loud voice, "Ouch! That hurt!" Then they laugh and vanish into thin air.

Ikuchi イクチ

TRANSLATION: none; just the name for this monster
ALTERNATE NAMES: ayakashi, ikuji
HABITAT: open seas
DIET: unknown; but it is big enough to eat anything it wants

APPEARANCE: Ikuchi are colossal sea monsters that roam the open seas off the coasts of Japan. They appear in numerous stories from the Edo period, where they are described as enormous fish or monstrous serpents of some kind. Their bodies are covered in a slippery oil, which sheds as they swim the ocean.

INTERACTIONS: When an ikuchi's path crosses a boat's, the sea monster envelopes the boat in its tentacle-like body. It slithers over the sides and across the deck, slowly sliding its whole body over the boat. Ikuchi are so long—many kilometers, by some accounts—that it can take hours for an entire one to slither over a boat. On a few occasions, boats have been tangled up in this monster for days. During this time, sailors must constantly bail the monster's oily slime off of the deck to avoid being capsized by the heavy goo.

ORIGIN: An ikuchi is depicted in Toriyama Sekien's bestiary *Konjaku Hyakki Shūi*, where it is called ayakashi. This yōkai is often referred to by that name. Ayakashi is more commonly used as a term for other strange creatures and supernatural phenomena and has nothing in particular to do with ikuchi. Toriyama Sekien may have just been listing the ikuchi as an example of an ayakashi. For whatever reason the name stuck.

UMI ZATŌ 海座頭

TRANSLATION: blind man of the sea
HABITAT: the waters surrounding Japan
DIET: prefers ships and sailors

APPEARANCE: Umi zatō are mysterious, gigantic yōkai that look like blind guildsmen, or *zatō*, who wander the seas at night. They tap the waves with their long canes.

INTERACTIONS: Very little is known about the mysterious umi zatō. They are considered to be harmless and leave people alone. However, according to some tales, umi zatō harass fishermen out at sea. They beckon ships towards them. When the ships draw close, they flip them over and capsize them. They occasionally swallow entire boats whole. They do have a congenial side, however. If the people on a ship reply to an umi zatō in a polite and docile manner, the umi zatō will vanish and leave them alone.

ORIGIN: Because there are so few legends about the umi zatō, almost all of what we know about them is speculation. They are sometimes considered to be cousins of the similar-looking umi bōzu, but it is likely that umi zatō is an invented yōkai thought up by Edo period artists solely for decorating picture scrolls.

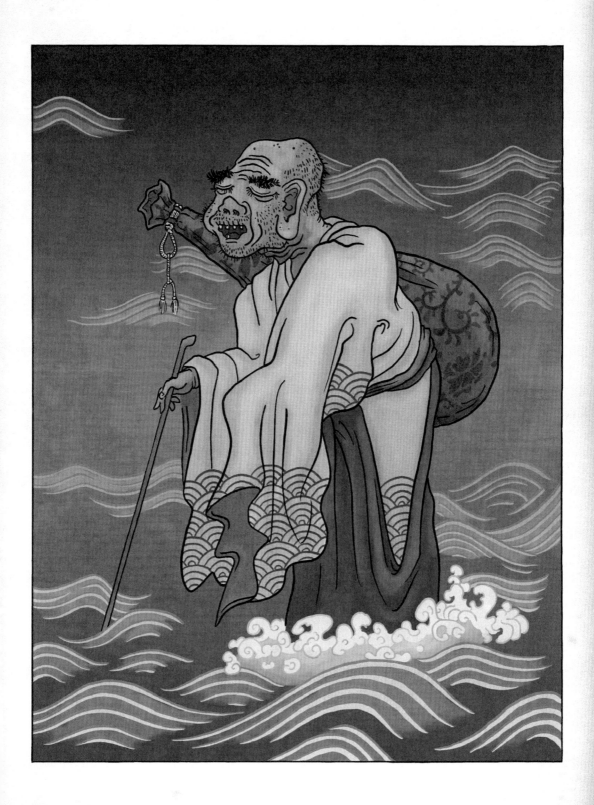

SAZAE ONI 栄螺鬼

TRANSLATION: turban snail demon
HABITAT: oceans, seas, and coastal areas
DIET: carnivorous

APPEARANCE: Sazae oni are monstrous turban snails (*Turbo cornutus*) which haunt the seas. They appear on moonlit nights, dancing on the water's surface like exotic dancers or dragons.

BEHAVIOR: Sazae oni are monstrous and deadly creatures, fully deserving the "demon" moniker. They are powerful shape-changers, often taking the form of beautiful women in order to lure seamen into trouble. At sea, they pretend to be drowning victims and cry out to be rescued. Then they turn on their would-be saviors once brought aboard. When encountered on land, sazae oni travel disguised as lone, wandering women who stop at inns. They eat the innkeepers during the night.

ORIGIN: Sazae oni can be born a few different ways. According to ancient lore, when animals reach a certain age they gain the ability to transform. It was thought that when a turban snail reaches 30 years old it turns into a yōkai with all kinds of magical powers. Another way that sazae oni come to be is when a lustful young woman is thrown into the sea. Such a woman transforms into a sea snail. If she happens to live a very long time, she transforms into a sazae oni as well.

LEGENDS: On the Kii peninsula, legend tells of a band of pirates who spotted a woman drowning in the water. They rescued her, though not out of the goodness in their hearts—the pirates had more nefarious reasons for wanting a woman aboard their ship. That night every pirate on the ship had their way with her. Unfortunately for the pirates, the woman was actually a shape-changed sazae oni. During the night, she visited each pirate on the boat one by one and bit off their testicles. At the end of the night she had all of their testicles, and demanded treasure for their return. The desperate pirates traded away all of their ill-gotten gold to the sazae oni to buy back their kintama, or "golden balls," as testicles are called in Japanese. In other words, they traded their gold for their gold.

SHINKIRŌ 蜃気楼

TRANSLATION: clam breath tower; mirage
HABITAT: open ocean

APPEARANCE: Shinkirō are not yōkai, but kaii—supernatural phenomenon. They take the appearance of distant, fantastic cities with tall towers and giant pagodas.

INTERACTIONS: Shinkirō appear out at sea on still nights, far off in the distance near the horizon. They only appear to sailors who are far from shore. Those who chase down these phantom cities never reach them. No matter how long they travel, the beautiful cities remain just as far away on the distant horizon.

ORIGIN: These mysterious illusions are caused by a legendary breed of giant clams, which breathe out fantastic images into the sky. These giant clams were known as *shin*, and were believed to be holy beasts related to dragons. Today, shinkirō remains a part of the Japanese lexicon as the word for mirage. While we understand the causes for this phenomenon today, its roots as a kaii are still preserved through the meaning of the kanji used to write the word: *shin* (clam), *ki* (breath), and *rō* (tower).

LEGENDS: According to legends, the mysterious cities that appears in these mirages are not just are illusory, but a vision of Ryūgū-jō, the mythical palace of Ryūjin—the dragon king who lives on the bottom of the sea.

RYŪJIN 龍神 AND RYŪGŪ-JŌ 龍宮城

While dragons are regarded as sacred beasts in Japanese lore, one dragon in particular is the grandest of all. Watatsumi, more commonly known as Ryūjin (meaning dragon god), is the god of all the oceans and seas and the king of the water spirits. He lives in a beautiful palace built from red and white corals called Ryūgū-jō, which sits at the bottom of the sea. From his palace, Ryūjin controls the oceans using the magical jewels kanju and manju, which cause the tides to ebb and flow. He is served by jellyfish, sea turtles, fish, and other marine life. In addition to water spirits and yōkai like kappa and suiko pay homage to Ryūjin.

Suiko 水虎

TRANSLATION: water tiger
ALTERNATE NAMES: sometimes mistakenly referred to as kappa
HABITAT: rivers, lakes, ponds and waterways; found throughout Japan
DIET: omnivorous; prefers human blood and souls

APPEARANCE: Suiko are found in both China and Japan and are often confused with kappa. However, suiko are far more dangerous, violent, and hot-tempered than their kappa cousins. Suiko have the body of a small child and are covered in tough scales like a pangolin's. They have sharp, hook-like growths on their kneecaps that resemble a tiger's claws. They live near riverbanks and large bodies of water.

BEHAVIOR: Suiko rank above kappa in the hierarchy of water goblins. They are sometimes placed in charge of kappa groups, with one suiko leading 48 kappa. They are sometimes called the oyabun, or yakuza bosses, of kappa. In turn, suiko report to Ryūjin, the dragon king, who lives in his palace Ryūgū-jō at the bottom of the sea. The main reason suiko attack humans is to look tougher than other suiko and increase their standing with the dragon king. Likewise, when kappa attack humans it makes them look tougher and increases their standing with their suiko bosses.

INTERACTIONS: Suiko live in inhabited areas and sneak out of the water at night to play pranks on humans. They knock on doors and run away, or possess people and make them do strange things. Like kappa and other water spirits, suiko use their superior strength to pull humans into water and drown them. Although unlike kappa, suiko have no concern for shirikodama. Instead, suiko drain their victims of blood like vampires. They then eat their souls (*reikon*) and return the drained body to the surface.

It is possible to keep suiko at bay by leaning a sickle against the side of your house and sprinkling flax seeds or black-eyed peas on the ground. Suiko are afraid of these and will keep away.

There is one known method to kill a suiko. It involves the corpse of a person who has had their blood drained by a suiko. First, you build a small hut made of grass and straw in a field. Then lay the drained body on a wooden plank and place it inside the hut. The suiko who sucked that person's blood will be drawn to the hut. It will run around and around in circles. Suiko are usually invisible, so it is likely that they will only be heard rather than seen. Only its footprints will be visible. As the dead body gradually decays, so will the suiko. By the time the body has rotted completely, the suiko will have died, its magic ceased. The decayed corpse of the suiko will become visible on the ground near the body.

SHIRANUI 不知火

TRANSLATION: unknown fire
HABITAT: along the shores of Kyūshū

APPEARANCE: Shiranui are a specific type of kaii known as a kaika, or mysterious fire. They appear in bodies of water around Kyūshū on dark, calm nights—particularly at the end of the 7th month according to the old lunar calendar. They are most visible during the strongest ebb tide, around 3 am, and appear roughly 8 to 12 kilometers off shore. They can be seen from elevated parts of the coast, but not from sea level.

BEHAVIOR: Shiranui begin with one or two distant fireballs, called *oyabi*, floating just above the surface of the sea. The oyabi sway left and right, splitting apart and multiplying until finally there are hundreds or thousands of fireballs swaying in the distance. This line of fireballs can stretch out for many kilometers.

ORIGIN: Shiranui were thought to be manifestations of the lanterns created by Ryūjin, the dragon god of the sea. On days that shiranui appeared, local villages were forbidden to catch fish in the same area as the kaika. Boats that tried approaching shiranui reported that no matter how long they sailed, the fireballs remained far away on the horizon.

Ryūtō 龍燈

TRANSLATION: dragon lights
HABITAT: oceans, coasts, lakes, rivers, and other bodies of water
DIET: none

APPEARANCE: Ryūtō are kaika which appear just above the surface of the water on calm, peaceful nights. They create no heat, nor do they burn anything. They are only found in bodies of water which are home to dragons.

BEHAVIOR: Ryūtō start out as single orbs of flame which hover a few meters above the surface of the water. They soon begin to multiply, until there are countless orbs. These fireballs float about aimlessly along the water, stretching and shrinking and morphing their shapes. Some of them sink back into the water. Others float up into the sky or nestle into the treetops. At dawn, they merge back together into one orb before vanishing back into the sea.

INTERACTIONS: Ryūtō are considered by the Japanese to be a manifestation of light caused by the dragons which inhabit bodies of water. Areas where ryūtō routinely appear often have shrines near them, and the lights themselves are considered sacred. On nights that ryūtō appear, people gather along the shore to watch these dancing and changing holy flames.

LEGENDS: The Itsukushima Shrine in Hiroshima Prefecture (old Bingo and Aki Provinces) is not only one of the most famous shrines in Japan, but also a popular sightseeing location for watching ryūtō. The lights appear on the tranquil surface of Hiroshima Bay for about a week starting on New Year's Day. They are believed to appear because the Itsukushima Shrine is dedicated to the gods of the sea and thus is connected with Ryūjin.

TENOME 手の目

TRANSLATION: eye hands
HABITAT: open fields and graveyards at night
DIET: human bones, fresh from the body

APPEARANCE: Tenome take the appearance of elderly zato, a kind of blind guildsman. Their faces have no eyes at all; instead, they have eyes on the palms of their hands.

BEHAVIOR: Tenome wander through open fields or graveyards at night, hunting for tasty humans. They wait until their prey is close before attacking. By the time you are able to recognize that you are face-to-face with not a zato but a tenome, it is too late. Tenome can run quickly. While their vision is not particularly strong they have a powerful sense of smell which helps them follow their victims in the dark.

ORIGIN: The tenome's true nature is not known. Most likely they are the ghosts of blind men who were robbed and murdered by thugs. This explanation can be traced to a folk tale, in which a man was attacked at night by a monster with eyes on its palms but none on its face. The victim fled to a nearby inn for shelter. He told the innkeeper what he saw, and the innkeeper replied that a few days earlier, a blind man was attacked and robbed out in that field. As the man lay dying in the grass, he cried out with his last breath, "If only I could have had once glance at their faces! If I only had eyes that worked—even on the palms of my hands...!" The old blind man's resent-filled death caused him to be reborn as a yōkai—with eyes on the palms of its hands and a heart full of hate.

LEGENDS: In Shichijō, Kyōto, a young man entered the graveyard at night as a test of his courage. From out of the darkness, a blind old man approached the young man. When the elderly figure got close enough to be seen in detail, the young man saw that it had eyeballs on the palms of his hands—and it was coming after him!

The young man ran as fast as he could to a nearby temple and begged the priest for sanctuary. The priest hid the man inside of a long chest and locked the lid. Shortly afterwards, the monster entered the temple, sniffing loudly as if it was hunting. The young man could hear the sniffing noise getting closer and closer, until it stopped right next to the chest he was hiding in. Then, there was a strange slurping sound, like the sound of a dog sucking on an animal's bones. A little while later, the eerie sounds vanished, and all was quiet. The priest opened up the chest to let the young man out, but all that was inside of the chest was the loose, empty skin of the young man. His bones had been completely sucked out of his body!

DODOMEKI 百々目鬼

TRANSLATION: hundred hundred eye (i.e. many-eyed) demon

APPEARANCE: Dodomeki are cursed women with very long arms covered in tiny bird eyes. They were once human girls who developed a penchant for stealing money. Because of their wicked actions, they transform into monsters—hundreds of tiny bird eyeballs sprout out of their arms.

ORIGIN: When Toriyama Sekien first described this yōkai, he inserted a number of puns. The dodomeki is described as being a woman with long arms. Having "long arms" in Japanese is a figure of speech meaning kleptomania. The dodomeki has long arms both figuratively and literally.

Copper coins, or *dōsen*, had holes in the middle of them. Because of this, they were colloquially known as a *chōmoku*, or "bird's eyes." This play on words is the reason dodomeki grow birds' eyes—a punishment for stealing copper coins.

Money was also sometimes referred to as *ashi*, or "feet," because it comes and goes as if it had its own feet. The phrase *ashi ga tsuku* is a common idiom which means "to catch someone who has committed a crime." Clever readers would notice that if the word ashi is replaced with chōmoku, the idiom changes to mean "covered in bird eyes."

LEGENDS: Long ago, in Shimotsuke Province, a demon had been sighted at a horse graveyard near Utsunomiya. A hero named Fujiwara no Hidesato grabbed his bow and arrow and went to investigate. Hidesato waited until nightfall. When the hour of the ox came, an enormous demon appeared and ravenously devoured the horse carcasses. The demon stood over ten feet tall and had sharp, spiked hair. It was covered in glowing eyes all over its body. Hidesato carefully aimed an arrow at the brightest glowing eyeball and fired. The arrow hit its mark, and the demon roared in pain. It fled into the woods until it collapsed at the foot of Mount Myōjin.

Although the demon was near-fatally wounded, it still had power left. From its body erupted a torrent of flames. Its mouth split open and poisonous fumes spewed forth. The toxic air and intense heat proved too much for Hidesato. He had to give up and return to his palace. When he returned the next day, the ground was blackened and burnt over a large area. There was no sign of the demon.

400 years later, a village had sprung up on the northern slope of Mount Myōjin. Strange things were happening there. The temple's head priest suffered mysterious injuries and unexplained fires broke out at the temple. A new head priest, the virtuous and holy Saint Chitoku, was called to discover what the cause of the strange problems was.

Saint Chitoku noticed a young woman who stopped by the temple frequently whenever he preached his sermons. He recognized her as the dodomeki in disguise. The wounded demon had retreated into some caves nearby to heal. It transformed into a young woman, and had been visiting the site where it fell. The village temple had been built on top of the battle site, and the dodomeki caused the fires and attacked the priest to scare them away. It was gradually sucking up all of the noxious fumes that it had breathed out, and collecting all of the blood that it had lost in its battle with Fujiwara no Hidesato.

Saint Chitoku confronted the disguised demon. It finally revealed its true form. The dodomeki did not attack him, however. While frequenting the temple, the dodomeki had overheard Chitoku's powerful sermons, and they had stuck with it. The dodomeki promised that it would never again commit any act of evil. Since then, the area around Mount Myōjin has come to be known as Dodomeki.

Tesso 鉄鼠

TRANSLATION: iron rat
DIET: feeds off of vengeance; also eats scrolls, books, statues, and holy relics

LEGENDS: Long ago, during the reign of Emperor Shirakawa (1073-1087 CE), there lived a monk named Raigō. He was the abbot of Mii-dera, a monastery in Ōmi Province at the foot of Mount Hiei, and well known for his piety.

The emperor, having no heir, was concerned about his line of succession. One day, he approached Raigō and asked him to pray to the gods and Buddha for an heir to the throne. Raigō prayed long and hard, and finally in 1074 Prince Taruhito was born. The grateful emperor promised to give the abbot anything he wished in return for his prayers. Raigō asked that a splendid new ordination building be constructed at Mii-dera so he could train new priests. The emperor gladly agreed. However, Mii-dera had a powerful rival—Enryaku-ji, on top of Mt. Hiei—which wielded influential political power as well as having a powerful army of warrior monks at its disposal. Enryaku-ji could not abide such a gift being granted to a rival temple, and pressured the emperor. Bowing to Enryaku-ji, the emperor reneged on his promise to Raigō.

Raigō began a hunger strike in protest of the emperor's broken promise. But the emperor would not—or could not—go against Enryaku-ji. On the 100th day of his hunger strike, Raigō passed away. As he died, his heart was full of rage towards the unfaithful emperor and the rival monastery of Enryaku-ji. So great was the hatred in Raigō's heart that he transformed into an onryō, a ghost driven by pure vengeance. Shortly after Raigō's death, a ghostly vision of the abbot was seen hovering near young Prince Taruhito's bed. A few days later the young prince died, leaving the emperor heir-less once again. Raigō's vengeance did not end there.

Raigō's twisted spirit transformed into a gigantic rat. Its body was as hard as stone and its teeth and claws as strong as iron. The monstrous spirit—Tesso as it came to be called—summoned an army of rats. They poured through Kyōto, up Mt. Hiei, and arrived at Enryaku-ji. There, the rats wreaked Raigō's vengeance. The army of rats poured through the monastery complex, chewing through the walls and doors, tearing up the roofs and floors, and attacking the monks. They devoured Enryaku-ji's precious sutras, scrolls, and books, eating and despoiling everything they found—they even ate the statues of the Buddha.

Nothing could stop Tesso and the army of rats until a shrine was built at Mii-dera to appease Raigō's spirit. Raigō's shrine still stands at Mii-dera today. An interesting footnote to the story: while Buddhist buildings are typically built facing the east, Raigō's shrine is built facing the north. It points to the top of Mt. Hiei, directly at Enryaku-ji, the target of his rage.

Amanozako 天逆毎

TRANSLATION: she who opposes everything in heaven
ALTERNATE NAMES: amanozako hime, onna tengu, metengu, tengu kami
HABITAT: heaven

APPEARANCE: Amanozako is a terrifying and powerful demon goddess. She is roughly human in appearance, but has a bestial face with a long, tengu-like nose, dangling ears, sharp teeth, and protruding tusks.

BEHAVIOR: Amanozako's hideous appearance is matched only by her foul, contrarian temper. She loves to go against the crowd, and does exactly the opposite of what is expected. She frequently possesses the hearts of humans, causing clever people to become overly proud and haughty, or foolish people to lose control over their tempers.

Amanozako is extremely picky and particular. When things do not go exactly the way she wants them to, she flies into a horrible rage. When angered, she can hurl even the most powerful gods distances of over one thousand villages in a single throw. Her powerful teeth can tear apart even the strongest blades. Nobody can stop her wrath.

ORIGIN: Amanozako was born from the temperamental storm god Susanoo. He had let his ferocious spirit and bad feelings build up inside of him until they formed into a large ball, which he eventually vomited up. That ball of ill-feeling became this goddess.

Stories about her are ancient, going back to long before recorded history. She is thought to be the ancestor deity of tengu, amanojaku, and other yōkai which share her penchant for disagreeability and short temper.

Amanozako has one son, Amanosaku. In keeping with her obstinate nature, she spawned him all by herself without any partner. Her son proved to be just as obstinate as she, and was such trouble that all eight million gods in heaven could not put up with him. Amanosaku was so terrible and disobedient that he was eventually made ruler over all the disobedient and malevolent kami.

Amanojaku 天邪鬼

TRANSLATION: heavenly evil spirits

ALTERNATE NAMES: amanjaku

APPEARANCE: Amanojaku are wicked monsters which have been known since before written history in Japan. They are described as evil kami, minor oni, or yōkai who cause mischief and perform evil deeds. In particular, they are known for provoking humans into acting upon the wicked, impious desires buried deep within their hearts. They spread spiritual pollution wherever they go.

ORIGIN: Although they predate Buddhism in Japan, amanjaku are frequently depicted in Buddhist imagery as symbols of wickedness being defeated by righteousness. In particular, the Four Heavenly Kings are depicted as standing on top of demons, squashing them—those squashed demons are said to be amanjaku. The god Bishamonten's armor is also decorated with demonic faces, which are said to be this evil spirit.

Amanojaku originate in ancient mythology. Though their true origins are a mystery, they appear to have developed out of ancient myths of wicked Shinto deities. Amanozako, Amenosagume, and Amenowakahiko all share aspects of this spirit's undermining nature. It is widely believed that amanjaku originated from one or even all of them.

LEGENDS: The most well-known tale about amanjaku is the story of Uriko hime. In this story, a childless elderly couple discovered a baby girl inside of a melon. They took her home and raised her as their own, and named her Uriko hime. She grew into a beautiful young woman, and one day a request for her hand in marriage arrived. Delighted, her parents went off to town to purchase her dowry and prepare for her wedding. Before leaving, they warned her not to open the door for anybody, no matter what!

Shortly afterwards, Uriko hime heard a knock at the door. "Uriko hime, please let me in!" She refused to open the door. The voice replied, "If you won't open the door, then at least open the window a crack..."

Reluctantly, Uriko hime opened the window just a crack. As soon as she had done so, a long, clawed finger slipped into the crack and smashed the window open. It was an amanjaku! The amanjaku leaped at Uriko hime, tearing at her clothes. The young woman fought for her life, biting and kicking at the demon, but she was not strong enough. The amanjaku snapped her neck, and she died.

The amanjaku didn't stop there, however. It flayed Uriko hime's skin and wore it like a suit, hiding itself in her clothes and disguising itself as the young girl. When the girl's parents came home, they were fooled into thinking their daughter was still alive.

Finally the wedding day arrived. The elderly couple brought the amanjaku-in-disguise to its husband-to-be. However, a crow in a nearby tree called out, warning the couple that their daughter was not what she seemed. They grabbed the bride tight and held her down. They washed her body until the flayed skin sloughed off, and the amanjaku was revealed.

The amanjaku ran for its life, but the elderly couple chased after it. More and more people joined them, until a whole host of villagers chased the demon through the village. Finally, the townspeople caught up to the amanjaku and hit it with sticks, stones, and tools. They beat the demon into a bloody mess, and it died.

Yamata no Orochi 八岐の大蛇

TRANSLATION: eight-branched serpent

DIET: omnivorous

APPEARANCE: Yamata no Orochi is a gigantic serpent with eight heads and eight tails. It has bright red eyes and a red belly. The beast is so large that its body covers the distance of eight valleys and eight hills. Fir and cypress trees grow on its back, and its body is covered in moss.

ORIGIN: Yamata no Orochi appears in the earliest written Japanese documents, the *Kojiki* and the *Nihongi*. Without a doubt, the legend goes back even farther into pre-history.

LEGENDS: Ages ago, the storm god, Susanoo, was thrown out of heaven and descended to earth at Mount Torikama near the Hi River in Izumo Province. There, he came upon an elderly couple of gods named Ashinazuchi and Tenazuchi, who were weeping. When Susanoo asked why they were crying, they explained that they once had eight daughters, but every year the eight-headed-eight-tailed serpent Yamata no Orochi demanded one as a sacrifice. They were now down to their eighth and final daughter, Kushinada hime. Soon it would be time for Yamata no Orochi to demand a sacrifice.

Susanoo explained that he was the elder brother of the sun goddess Amaterasu, and offered to slay the beast in return for Kushinada hime's hand in marriage. The elderly couple agreed, and Susanoo set in motion his plan to defeat the serpent.

First, Susanoo transformed Kushinada hime into a comb, which he placed in his hair. Then, he had Ashinazuchi and Tenazuchi build a large fence with eight gates. On each gate they raised a platform and on each platform they placed a vat. They poured extremely strong sake into each vat. When this was finished, everyone waited for the serpent to arrive.

When Yamata no Orochi appeared, the great serpent slithered into the fence and noticed the powerful sake. It dipped its eight heads into the vats and drank the alcohol. Soon, the monster fell into a deep, drunken sleep. Susanoo used this chance to make his attack. He sliced the enormous beast into tiny pieces with his sword. The carnage was so great that the Hi River flowed with blood. When Susanoo had cut the creature down to its fourth tail, his sword shattered into pieces. Examining the part of Yamata no Orochi's tail which broke his sword, Susanoo discovered another sword within the creature's flesh: the legendary katana Kusanagi no Tsurugi.

Susanoo eventually offered Kusanagi as a gift to his sister, Amaterasu, and was allowed to return to heaven. The sword was passed down through the generations in the imperial line of Japan. It is one of the three pieces of imperial regalia, along with the mirror Yata no Kagami and the jewel Yasakani no Magatama. Today, the sword which came from Yamata no Orochi's tail is said to be safeguarded in the Atsuta Shrine in Nagoya.

MEIDO 冥途

TRANSLATION: dark way; the underworld

APPEARANCE: When someone dies, they either go to Tengoku (heaven) or Jigoku (hell). If they lived an exceptionally good or an exceptionally evil life, they may go straight to Tengoku or Jigoku. However, for most people—who have done both and good and evil in their lives—the soul travels to Meido. There they face a test by the judges of the dead, each of whose true form is that of a buddha or a god. They are then sent either to Tengoku or Jigoku. Meido is a terrible place—though nowhere near as terrible as Jigoku. It is dark, windy, and full of horrible sights, sounds, tests and trials. It is a long journey, with no place to rest or find comfort.

To enter the underworld, the soul much first find and cross the Sanzu River, the River of Three Crossings, which marks the boundary between this world and the world of the dead. The Sanzu River is said to be located somewhere on Mount Osore, literally Mount Fear, a desolate volcano located in northern Japan. Despite its appearance—covered in blasted rocks, bubbling pits of dark liquid, and open vents spewing out toxic gas—Mount Osore is one of the three holiest places in Japan. Itako, blind shamanesses, communicate with the dead as they approach the mountain. The itako take hallucinogenic mushrooms known as skull mushrooms (ōdokurodake—big skull mushrooms; himedokurodake—princess skull mushrooms; and onidokurodake—demon skull mushrooms) which sprout only on the crags of this caldera.

INTERACTIONS: There are many variations on what exactly happens after this life ends. These are often depicted in graphic hell scrolls kept at temples. The depictions differ greatly from tradition to tradition and place to place. A typical explanation may go like this:

Upon dying, souls are visited by three oni who escort them on a seven day journey to Meido. The journey is harsh and terrible. It is dark, and a strong, howling wind rages constantly. The corruption of the living world materializes into swords on this plane, which pierce the bodies of the travelers, turning the surrounding terrain into a sea of blood.

A few days along the way, the souls are assaulted by horrible birds, which tear at their skin and pluck out their eyes. All the while the birds taunt them and scream at them to hurry up. "Why didn't you tell me sooner? I would have hurried from the start!" cry the souls of the dead. "What is this stupid soul saying!" cry the birds. "We were perched on his roof since three days before he died, warning him to start saying his prayers! That fool only said, 'The crows are being extra noisy today. The old woman next door must be dying. Go bring her some sugar.' Well the old woman is still alive, happily licking her sugar!"

Next, the souls come to an enormous mountain which scrapes the clouds, covered in sharp thorns. The path up the mountain is steep and impossibly long. The souls cry out, "I was sick and weak in life, how can you expect me to climb such a mountain now?" To which the oni reply, "What is this stupid soul saying! This is the mountain of your greed! Every time you wanted something your neighbor owned, or desired some earthly possession, you added to this mountain! You built it, now you can climb it!" Anyone who lags behind gets hit with the oni's terrible iron club.

Finally, after seven days, the souls arrive at the Sanzu River and face the first trial put forth by the first judge, King Shinkō (whose true form is that of Fudō Myōō; who is known as Acala in English). Shinkō judges the souls on how much killing they have committed, down to every bug that was squashed and every fish that was caught. Those whom Shinkō judges to be wicked go straight to Jigoku. Others may cross the river depending on how well they fared in the trial. To cross the Sanzu River, a toll of 6 mon (an old form of currency) is required. This is buried with

the deceased during the funeral. Those whose funerals were not properly performed and did not receive the 6 mon cannot cross. This is the reason that the seventh day after death is an important day in Japanese funerary services. The services and prayers performed for the deceased aid them in this trial and allow them to cross the river.

One part of the Sanzu River is crossed by a great bridge. Another part of the river is shallow and fordable. The rest of the river is wild and deep, and filled with poisonous snakes. The souls with the most good deeds are allowed to cross the bridge. Those with a mixture of both good and evil may ford the river in the shallow part. The worst of the souls may only cross by swimming through snake-filled rapids. The crossing of the Sanzu River takes seven days.

After crossing the river, the souls encounter Datsueba and Ken'eō. These two oni take the heavy clothes from each soul, wet from the crossing of the river, and hang them on a tree. The amount the branch bends under the weight of the clothes serves as a measure of the weight of the sin on each soul, to be used as evidence in the trials to come. If a soul arrives with no clothes—perhaps having discarded them while swimming in the river—Datsueba flays his or her skin and hangs it from the tree instead.

The second trial takes place fourteen days after death, and is overseen by King Shokō (whose true form is Shaka Nyōrai, or Siddhartha Gautama). Shokō judges the souls on how much they have stolen. As with the previous trial, he sends the most grievous offenders straight to hell, while allowing the good to pass on to the next trial. Again, the fourteenth day after death is an important day for family members to perform ceremonies in honor of the deceased, in order to help him or her pass this trial.

Before the third trial, each soul must pass through a fortified gate which is guarded by a fierce oni. The oni wields large blades, which he uses to haphazardly chop off the arms and legs of the souls, saying, "That hand helped you to sin. I'll cut if off for you!" The souls must then cross an enormous bay, wider than the Sanzu River, and filled with boiling liquid. The river gives off foul smelling fumes in all directions for many miles.

The third trial takes place 21 days after death, and is overseen by King Sōtei (whose true form is Manji Bosatsu, or Manjusri). Sōtei judges the souls on their sins of lust and sexuality, using a cat and a snake. The cat judges the souls of men; it bites at their penises, and the degree of the injury—from a slight scratch to completely severed—is used as a measure of one's sexual sin. The snake judges the souls of women; it is inserted into the woman, and the depth to which it can enter is used to determine the depth of her sin. As before, some will go on to hell, while others—with the aid of funerary services from their surviving family members—will pass on to the next trial.

The fourth trial, 28 days after death, is overseen by King Gokan (whose true form is Fugen Bosatsu, or Samantabhadra). Gokan judges the dead on the number of lies they told in life. He weighs each soul against a large, heavy stone. The number of stones it takes the balance the scale determines the weight of one's sins. Excessive liars are damned—those who are not may continue on to be judged again. Once again, the family holds a funerary service to aid their beloved departed in this trial, hoping to sway the mercy of the judge.

Next, the souls must cross a vast blasted, desolate landscape of unfathomable length. Balls of red-hot iron fall constantly like rain from the sky, burning the skin of the souls and causing their feet to blister as they walk the path to the next trial.

The fifth trial, 35 days after death, is overseen by Great King Enma, the ruler of the underworld (whose true form is that of Jizō Bosatsu, or Ksitigarbha). Enma's judgment is the final chance to appeal one's fate through the prayers and memorial services performed by the living relatives.

Enma shows each soul a large mirror, in which the individual's former life is reflected back at them, with all of their sins and transgressions clearly laid out. Enma's job is to decide, based on his and the previous trials, which of the six Buddhist realms each soul will be reborn into: the realm of heaven, the realm of humans, the realm of ashura, the realm of beasts, the realm of gaki (or hungry ghosts), or the realm of hell.

After 42 days, the souls which have made it this far now face the judgment of King Henjō (whose true form is Miroku Bosatsu, or Maitreya). Henjō decides the location of each soul's rebirth based on the reports from Enma's mirror and Gokan's scale.

Next, the souls must cross a dark land, full of strange animals whose cries pierce the darkness and fill the atmosphere with dread. Strange birds attack the souls, breathing flames at them and piercing them with their sharp beaks.

On the 49th day after death, the souls reach the trial of King Taizan (whose true form is Yakushi Nyōrai, or Bhaisajyaguru). The 49th day memorial service is an important one, with many family members attending to pray for the deceased; Taizan's trial is the final chance to avoid going to hell. He uses the information from the previous judges to determine the remaining conditions of each soul's rebirth.

Upon completion of this trial, each soul moves on to a road with six unmarked torii gates, each representing one of the Buddhist realms. There is no way to tell which gate leads to which realm, and each soul must decide for him or herself which gate to choose. Upon passing through the gate, the soul travels along an enormous frozen river, and leaves Meido for the next world, whichever one it may be. For many, the journey ends here. Those who have been judged worthy may find themselves in Tengoku. Others are reborn as humans, animals, or worse. For those deemed unworthy for even the lowest forms of rebirth, more trials await in the realm of Jigoku.

ORIGIN: The origins of Meido are strongly rooted in Chinese Buddhism. When Buddhism was brought from India to China it took on a structure of its own, merging many aspects with Chinese philosophy and Taoism. This mixture of Chinese Taoism and Indian Buddhism was imported to Japan, after which it began to develop its own uniquely Japanese features as well.

JIGOKU 地獄

TRANSLATION: earth prison; hell

APPEARANCE: Souls who are deemed unworthy of rebirth in the five upper Buddhist realms find themselves in the worst afterlife of all—Jigoku, or Buddhist hell. Though it is described as one realm, Jigoku is not just one place. There are countless different hells, which are usually separated into eight hot hells and eight cold hells. These are further subdivided into many other smaller planes and demi-planes—more than 64,000 according to some counts—and each one has a uniquely specialized form of punishment and length of stay, tailor-made to the sins of its inhabitants. While there are many different levels of hell in Japanese Buddhism, the general term Jigoku usually refers to the eight hot hells, also known as the eight great hells. The eight great hells are as follows:

Tōkatsu Jigoku, the reviving hell, is the plane of hell reserved for those who commit the sin of killing. Those who kill without remorse go to this hell. Even the killing of lesser creatures such as mosquitoes, flies, or ants—unless repented—will cause a soul to go to this hell. In addition, people who were particularly pugilistic in life, and those who died in mutiny or uprisings will also fall into this hell. Here, the ground is ever hot and burning. Denizens of this hell must fight each other with iron claws, tearing each other to pieces. Terrible oni roam the land, smashing, and pulverizing souls with their iron clubs. As soon as a soul dies, a cool breeze blows and it is instantly revived, and must fight to the death again. Souls here experience the pain of being killed countless times, for a life span in the reviving hell lasts 500 years. However, time in hell is measured differently than in the world of the living: one day in this hell is equivalent to 500 years in the realm of the Four Heavenly Kings, while one day there is equivalent to 50 years on earth. Therefore, a soul in Tōkatsu Jigoku must continue this punishment for over 1.6 trillion human years.

Kokujō Jigoku, the hell of black threads, is reserved for those who have not only killed but also committed the sin of theft. Here, oni knock the souls onto the hot ground and mark lines on their body with black threads. Then, using axes and saws, the bodies are hacked to pieces along the markings made by the threads. Others are made to carry heavy piles of hot iron across a tightrope suspended over a giant frying pan. When the victims fall, they are boiled and hacked to pieces in the pan. One life span here lasts a thousand years; however, a day in this hell is equivalent to 1000 years in the realm of Tōriten, while one day in Tōriten is equivalent to 100 years in the human realm. This works out to about 13.3 trillion human years.

Shugō Jigoku, the crushing hell, is reserved for sinners who have killed, stolen, and also committed the sin of lewdness. The suffering here is ten times greater than that of Kokujō Jigoku. Denizens here are crushed repeatedly between mountains of iron, being pulverized into a bloody jelly. When the mountains separate, life is restored and the process begins again. Trees with razor-like leaves dot the landscape, and beautiful men and women beckon to the souls from the tree tops. The lustful inhabitants climb the trees, slicing their bodies up in the process, and when they reach the treetops the beautiful men and women reappear at the bottoms of the trees, beckoning them back down. As blood and severed organs spout from the bodies, giant demons and beasts rush in to gobble of their entrails and pound the souls into a bloody mush. Fellators have their tongues stretched out and nailed to their ears. Pedophiles have molten copper pumped into their anuses until it pours out of their mouths. Homosexuals see their lovers covered in flames, and are forced to embrace them, only to be burned and torn into pieces themselves. Souls remain here for 2000 years; however, one day here lasts 2000 years in the realm of Yamaten, and one day in Yamaten lasts 200 human years. Thus, a lifetime here is equivalent to over 106 trillion human years.

Kyōkan Jigoku, the screaming hell, is for murders, thieves, lechers, and alcoholics. The suffering

here is ten times stronger than in the previous hell. Here, sinners are thrown into boiling pots or locked up in iron chambers and roasted by oni. Those who committed crimes while drunk have their mouths wrenched open and molten iron is poured into their bellies. The cries of anguish of the denizens only serve to anger the oni further, and they fire arrows at the souls or bash them with iron clubs to make them stop, at which point they only revive and resume their suffering. One lifetime here lasts 4,000 years, of which one day is equal to 4,000 years in Tosotsuten, of which one day is equal to 400 human years. Thus, a condemned soul will spend over 852 trillion years in Kyōkan Jigoku.

Daikyōkan Jigoku, the hell of great screaming, contains murderers, thieves, debauchers, drunks, and liars. The suffering inflicted here is ten times worse than in the previous hell. Here, the tongues of the damned are pierced with iron nails and stretched and torn from their bodies, after which they grow back and are immediately pierced and torn again. This continues for 8,000 years, one day of which equals 8,000 years in Kerakuten, where one day is equivalent to 800 human years. The damned in Daikyōkan Jigoku suffer for an equivalent of roughly 6.8 quadrillion years.

Jōnetsu Jigoku, the burning hell, contains killers, robbers, perverts, drunkards, liars, and those who have held thoughts or beliefs contrary to Buddhist teachings. Here, the tortured souls are beaten with red-hot iron clubs. They have hot skewers thrust through their mouths and out their anuses, and are broiled over a great sea of fire. A life span in this hell lasts 16,000 years, one day of which equals 16,000 years in Takejizaiten, where one day is equivalent to 1,600 years on earth. A damned soul here spends the equivalent of 54.5 quadrillion human years.

Daijōnetsu Jigoku, the hell of great burning, is much the same as Jōnetsu Jigoku, only much hotter. The suffering here is equivalent to ten times more than all of the higher hells combined. This plane of hell is reserved for sinners who have committed all of the crimes listed previously in addition to physical crimes against Buddhist clergy—for example, raping a nun. The screams of the tortured souls here are so terrible that they can be heard up to 24,000 miles away. The power of this hell is so great that those who are to be sentenced here begin to feel their suffering up to three days before they actually die. The punishment on this level of hell lasts one half of an antarakalpa—a unit of time in Indian cosmology that is so unfathomably long that it defies mathematical description.

Mugen Jigoku, the hell of uninterrupted suffering, is the eighth and deepest circle of hell. It is reserved for the worst of the worst—murders of their own parents; killers of saints; those who have betrayed every single Buddhist precept. The souls down here are so hungry and thirsty that they tear apart their own bodies and drink their own blood in a useless attempt to ease their suffering. Words literally cannot describe how awful this hell is; if Mugen Jigoku were ever accurately described, both the reader and the writer would die from the sheer horror of it. It is so deep that it takes 2000 years of falling, non-stop, at terminal velocity, for a soul to descend all the way into this hell. Some say that those who are sent here never come back, while others say that the term of punishment here lasts one full antarakalpa, after which the soul may reincarnate again; although, even after a soul is finally released from this hell, its punishment is said to continue on into its next lives.

INTERACTIONS: Because Jigoku is so terrible and the buddhas so merciful, the tortured souls in Jigoku are allowed a few more trials like the ones they received in Meido to see whether they can be released from hell early or not—or at least have their existence "upgraded" to a less torturous one. On specific days, Buddhist memorial services are held by the deceased's surviving relatives. While the specifics of what exactly happens in Jigoku vary between different Buddhist traditions, this is one explanation of the trials:

100 days after death marks the first trial in Jigoku. These trials are not so much judgments, as the soul is already being tortured in hell. They are more like appeals, where the soul (and his or her still-living family) get to appeal to the gods and the buddhas for one more chance at salvation. During the first of these trials, the soul is brought before King Byōdō (whose true form is Kannon Bosatsu, also known as Guanyin or Avalokitesvara in English).

On the 1 year anniversary of the death, the soul is once again brought to trial. This time the judge is King Toshi (whose true form is Seishi Bosatsu, or Mahasthamaprapta).

On the 2nd year anniversary of one's death (the beginning of the third year after death), the soul is granted another chance for salvation by trial. King Godō-tenrin (whose true form is Amida Nyōrai, or Amitabha) presides over this judgment. In Chinese Buddhism, this tenth trial is the last chance for salvation; however, in some forms of Japanese Buddhism the soul still gets three more chances for salvation from Jigoku.

The next trial occurs 6 years after death, and is presided over by King Renge (whose true form is Ashuku Nyōrai, or Akshobhya).

Another trial occurs 12 years after death, and is presided over by King Gion (whose true form is Dainichi Nyōrai, or Vairocana).

The thirteenth and final trial occurs 32 years after death. This last trial is presided over by King Houkai (whose true form is Kokūzō Bosatsu, or Akasagarbha). Those who fail all three of these final tests, either through their own faults or from lack of prayers by their living relatives, are damned to remain in hell for a very, very long time before they can be reborn into one of the five other realms.

ORIGIN: Like Meido, the Japanese concept of Jigoku derives from Chinese Buddhism—specifically the concept of Diyu, which is in turn derived from the Indian Buddhist concept of Naraka. After being imported to Japan from China, it developed other uniquely Japanese features, although it never merged with the native Shinto concept of hell, Yomi.

ENMA DAIŌ 閻魔大王

TRANSLATION: Great King Enma

HABITAT: Jigoku and Meido

APPEARANCE: Enma Daiō is the ruler of hell (both Jigoku and Meido) and the foremost of the 13 judges of the dead. He has dresses in the robes of an ancient government official from the Chinese Tang Dynasty, and wears a fearsome expression upon his face. He is served by two secretaries, Shiroku and Shimyō, as well as a number of other demonic servants—the chiefs of which are Gozu and Mezu. His name often is invoked by parents who scold their children, "If you tell a lie, Enma will rip out your tongue!"

BEHAVIOR: Enma's chief duty is to judge the souls of the newly dead and send them on to their next location. He keeps a great scroll in which he records all of the good and evil deeds of each and every person to use as evidence against them when their time of judgment comes. He oversees the torturing and suffering in hell, making sure that each soul gets enough punishment.

ORIGIN: Like many demonic figures in Japanese folklore, Great King Enma has a honji, or "true form," which is that of a Buddha or bodhisattva. Enma's true form is Jizō Bosatsu, the guardian of the underworld, god of travelers, and protector of children. Jizō is a warm and compassionate, beloved across Japan, deity who made a solemn vow not to become a full Buddha until all souls have been freed from suffering in hell. It is not uncommon to see small, red-bibbed, stone Jizō statues along roads and paths, and in graveyards all over Japan. While Enma may seem fearsome and terrifying, at heart, he is a kind and compassionate god, and he truly wishes to save each soul from damnation—this may be why the souls of the dead are given so many tests and trials to avoid going to hell.

Enma's origins lie in India. In Vedic mythology he is known as Yama, the god of death. From the Vedas, the idea of Yama spread into Hinduism, Sikhism, and Buddhism. Buddhism traveled to China, bringing Yama with it, and mixed with local religions and superstitions before being brought to Japan during the Tang Dynasty. As Chinese Buddhism mixed with Japanese religions and superstitions, he gradually developed into the god known as Great King Enma.

HOLIDAYS IN HELL

Enma's holy days fall on the 16th day of each month. The first and seventh month are particularly important to him, and on these days, he and his servants take off from work and return to their homes. On these days, temples and shrines dedicated to Enma display statues and flags in honor of Enma, and prayers and offerings made on these holidays are said to provide much more merit than those offered on ordinary days. Temples dedicated to him frequently serve konnyaku treats to guests on these days, as konnyaku is Enma's favorite food.

In addition, the first day of the seventh month (by the old lunar calendar—this generally translates to mid-August by today's calendar) is a holiday for all of Jigoku, called *Kamabuta Tsuitachi*, "Kettle Lid First Day of the Month." On this day, the lids of all of the boiling cauldrons are opened up and the souls are allowed a brief reprieve from torture. This day also marks the beginning of the Obon season, when the dead return from the afterlife to be with their families. The tortured souls in hell crawl out from their boiling pots, cages, and so on, and make the long journey to the world of the living, returning to hell after Obon to resume their torture.

Datsueba 奪衣婆

TRANSLATION: clothes-stealing old woman
ALTERNATE NAMES: sōzukaba, ubason

Ken'eō 懸衣翁

TRANSLATION: clothes-hanging old man
HABITAT: Meido, along the banks of the Sanzu River

APPEARANCE: Datsueba and Ken'eō are a terrifying pair of elderly oni. They guard the bridge and the banks of the Sanzu River. All souls must pass by them before moving on to Meido to be judged.

INTERACTIONS: During a Japanese funeral, 6 *mon* (and old form of currency) are placed in the coffin to be used as a toll to enter the underworld. Upon reaching the Sanzu River, the souls must cross either by bridge (if they were good in life), by wading in the shallows (if they were only somewhat good), or by swimming across the deepest part of the river (if they were wicked).

After crossing the river, each soul encounters Datsueba, who accepts the toll and strips the souls of the clothes on their backs. Datsueba hands the clothing to her partner, Ken'eō, who hangs it from a tree by the riverside. The amount that the branch bends under the weight of the clothes serves as a measure of the weight of the sin each soul carries, and is used as evidence in the trials to come. Of course, the clothes of those who had to ford the river or swim across are heavy and wet, which only makes the branches of the tree sag lower. If a soul arrives with no clothes, Ken'eō flays his or her skin and hangs it from the tree instead.

Datsueba and Ken'eō perform a little bit of torture themselves, breaking the fingers of those guilty of theft, and so on. They also roam the banks of the river, tormenting the souls of children who are too young to cross the river and must wait for salvation to come to them instead.

According to some accounts, Datsueba is the wife of King Enma. In the Edo period, she became a popular object of folk worship, and temples dedicated to her began to spring up around Japan. Prayers and charms dedicated to Datsueba were used as wards against disease and coughs, in particular for children's coughs.

Sai no Kawara

The souls of children are not allowed to cross the Sanzu River. Instead, they are forced to sit on the riverbanks in a sort of limbo called Sai no Kawara. Their souls remain in Sai no Kawara until enough prayers have been said for them to earn enough merit to cross. Here they sit, building towers out of pebbles, adding one pebble each time someone says a prayer for them. When a tower is completed, the child can finally cross; however, Datsueba and Ken'eō roam the banks and constantly knock the pebble towers over, rendering the effort meaningless. The only way for children to leave Sai no Kawara is to be saved through intercession by Jizō Bosatsu, the guardian deity of children. This is why Jizō is such a popular god in Japan; prayers to him go towards saving the souls of lost children.

Gozu 牛頭

TRANSLATION: ox head
ALTERNATE NAMES: gozuki (ox head demon)

Mezu 馬頭

TRANSLATION: horse head
ALTERNATE NAMES: mezuki (horse head demon)
HABITAT: Meido and Jigoku

APPEARANCE: In Japanese Buddhism, Gozu and Mezu are the demon generals who guard the gates of hell. They appear as terrible oni with animal heads; an ox head for Gozu, and a horse head for Mezu. They are extremely powerful and have the strength to move mountains. They are servants of Great King Enma, the ruler of hell, and are among the chief torturers and punishers of the wicked.

INTERACTIONS: Gozu and Mezu are the first demons that one encounters upon entering hell. Should a person manage to escape from hell, Gozu and Mezu are sent out to bring them back.

ORIGIN: Though Gozu and Mezu are the most famous and most commonly depicted in story and art, they are not the only animal-headed demons in Great King Enma's employ. Deer, tiger, lion, and boar-headed demons are also said to serve among the upper ranks of the guardians of hell. They operate the great torture chambers of Jigoku and oversee the torment of countless souls. Gozu, Mezu, and other animal-headed demons originate in Indian mythology, which was imported along with Buddhism to Japan by way of China.

ASHURA 阿修羅

TRANSLATION: asura; warrior demons from Buddhist cosmology
ALTERNATE NAMES: asura
HABITAT: Ashuradō, one of the celestial realms
DIET: carnivorous; they thrive on violence and destruction

APPEARANCE: Ashura are fearsome demon gods with multiple faces and arms. They are roughly human-like in appearance, though their size, strength, and numerous appendages distinguish them from mere mortals.

BEHAVIOR: Ashura are warriors above all else, and live for battle. They love combat, war, and destroying things. They have enormous egos; ashura always desire to be better than others, have no patience for those weaker than they are, and prefer to solve any problem with violence.

There are many different kinds of ashura. Some are considered to be gods and others demons. Ashura are strong, powerful, and magical. In many ways they are far superior to humans. They experience more pleasure than those in the human realm, and live much longer. However, they are controlled by such intense passions—wrath, pride, violence, and greed—that despite their pleasure-filled existence they are constantly fighting and never at peace. Ashura are also wracked with jealousy; to be reborn as an ashura means to be constantly reminded how much better life would have been if you had been reborn in a heavenly realm instead of Ashuradō.

ORIGIN: In Japanese Buddhism, after someone dies, they are eventually reborn in one of the 6 Buddhist realms: Tendō, the realm of heaven; Ningendō, the realm of humans; Ashuradō, the realm of ashura, Chikushōdō, the realm of animals; Gakidō, the realm of hungry ghosts; and Jigokudō, the realm of hell. Of these, only two realms are considered to be "happy" rebirths—the heavenly realm and the human realm. Of the remaining realms, the realm of Jigoku is the worst, followed by Gakidō. The realm of animals is not a good rebirth because animals are ruled by their desires and thus cannot obtain enlightenment. Ashuradō, the realm of the ashura, is the least unpleasant of the "unhappy" rebirths.

In some Buddhist traditions, the realm of ashura is considered to be the lowest level of heaven, and gets included among the "happy" rebirths. However, because ashura are so controlled by their emotions, it is almost impossible for them to achieve enlightenment, become buddhas, and escape the cycle of endless reincarnation. Souls who are reborn here are usually humans who lived good lives up to a point, but committed some wicked deed which prevents them from being reborn in the realm of heaven.

GAKI 餓鬼

TRANSLATION: hungry ghosts, preta; suffering spirits from Buddhist cosmology
HABITAT: Gakidō, a realm of suffering, starvation, and thirst
DIET: gaki will try to eat anything, but are never able to find nourishment

APPEARANCE: Gaki are spirits which live in horrible torment and are afflicted with constant suffering. They look vaguely human, but they have distended, bulging bellies and tiny, inefficient mouths and throats. They inhabit a parallel realm called Gakidō. It is a barren place, full of deserts, wastelands, and other inhospitable terrain.

BEHAVIOR: Gaki are eternally hungry and thirsty. There are many kinds of gaki, each of which suffers in a different way related to the sins he or she committed in a past life. Some are unable to eat or drink anything at all. Whenever they try to eat, the food instantly bursts into flames and vanishes. These gaki are only able to eat food which has been specially blessed for them in Buddhist services. Some gaki are able to eat only unclean things, such as feces, vomit, corpses, and so on. Others have no trouble eating anything they please. However, no matter how much they wolf down, their hunger and thirst are never sated.

INTERACTIONS: In some Buddhist traditions, a special ceremony called *segaki* is performed during the Obon season, to help ease the suffering of the gaki. In this ceremony, offerings of rice and water are laid out on special altars, out of sight of any statues of the gods or Buddha. The gaki are called to come and eat, while prayers are said to ease some of their suffering.

ORIGIN: The realm of the gaki is considered one of the four "unhappy" rebirths. In the cosmology of birth and rebirth, the realm of the gaki is only one step above the realm of Jigoku—the main difference between the inhabitants of Jigoku and the gaki being that those in Jigoku are confined to their prison. Gaki may roam free as they suffer.

Today, the word gaki is also a very nasty term for a child. This comes from the perception of children always wanting more food and never feeling satisfied with what they get.

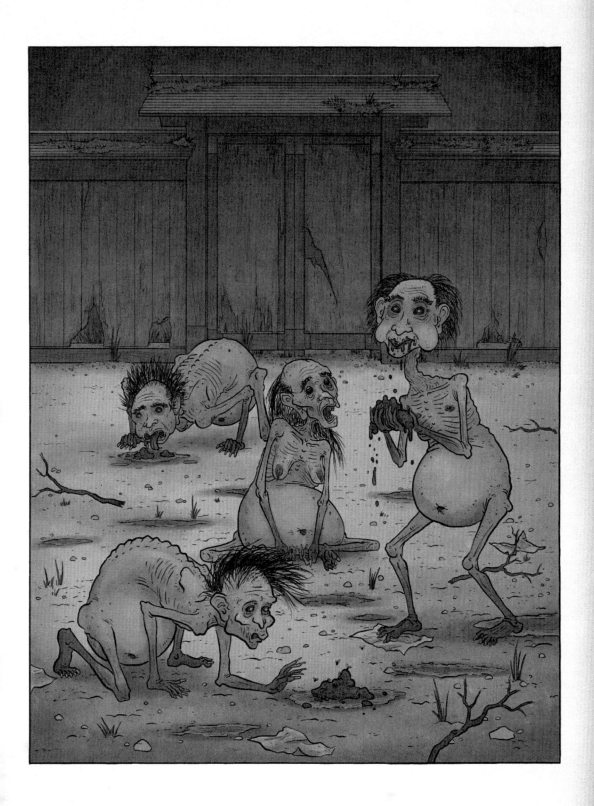

ONO NO TAKAMURA 小野篁

APPEARANCE: Ono no Takamura was a noble, scholar, poet, and government official who lived in the first half of the 9th century. He is famous for being clever, quick-witted, and somewhat insolent. But he is even more famous for his side job in hell as an attendant to Great King Enma.

LEGENDS: Near the temple Rokudōchinnō-ji in Kyōto, there is a spot where the boundary between the world of the dead and the world of the living can be crossed. There are many stories in that area of ghosts returning to this world and trying to buy candy from stores, or visiting lost relatives. Ono no Takamura knew of this, and discovered a way to travel freely between the world of the dead and the world of the living. He would enter the underworld every night by climbing down a well located in the garden of Rokudōchinnō-ji, and return every morning by climbing out of a well located in the temple Sagano Fukusei-ji.

According to one legend, a nobleman named Fujiwara no Yoshimi fell very ill and died soon after. His soul crossed the Sanzu River, and traveled to Meido to be judged. When he reached the court of King Enma, a familiar voice spoke up from the darkness next to the judge and said, "I know this soul. In life, he served as an imperial minister, and was a noble and virtuous man. Please trust my judgment and return him to life." When Yoshimi raised his head, he saw that the voice belonged to Ono no Takamura—and he was serving as one of King Enma's councilors! King Enma replied, "Well, if you say so I suppose it can't be helped," and ordered his hell-guards to return Yoshimi to the world of the living.

A few days later, Fujiwara no Yoshimi approached Ono no Takamura at the imperial court. When Yoshimi asked Takamura about what he saw in Meido, Takamura appeared troubled and replied, "My work there is actually a secret, so please don't tell anybody else about what you saw..." Afterwards, Yoshimi began to grow more and more fearful of Takamura's power and position. Rumors spread through the capital that Takamura was King Enma's right hand man. Many feared him.

Rokudōchinnō-ji still stands in Kyōto today. In the Enma Hall, right next to the statue of Great King Enma is another statue—one of Ono no Takamura. The well which Takamura used to enter the world of the dead still remains on the temple garden; however Sagano Fukusei-ji no longer stands, and the place where Takamura's exit well once stood is now a bamboo forest.

Kowai 狐者異

TRANSLATION: strange fox person; origin of the word for "scary"
HABITAT: food stalls, garbage dumps
DIET: any scrap of food it can get its hands on

APPEARANCE: Kowai are the ghosts of gluttonous people who carried their obsessions with food into death, transforming into this yōkai. They take the form of grotesque humans with blood-shot eyes, sharp teeth, fox-like features, and long, drooling tongues. They appear at night outside of food stands and restaurants.

BEHAVIOR: Kowai are concerned with only one thing—eating. They always suffer from hunger, and ravenously devour any bit of food they can get their claws on. They rifle through garbage pales, knock down food stalls, and attack food vendors late at night. They wolf down whatever scraps have been left behind. Kowai will even pick at carrion in the streets. No matter how spoiled or how disgusting, if it can be eaten, a kowai will go after it.

ORIGIN: Kowai first appear in the *Ehon Hyakumonogatari*, an encyclopedia of ghosts published in 1841. Their name is written with kanji meaning "fox," "person," and "strange," and can literally be translated as "weird fox person." According to that book, kowai are the origin of the word 怖い (*kowai*), which means "scary" in Japanese.

Amefuri kozō 雨降小僧

TRANSLATION: rainfall priest boy
HABITAT: found throughout Japan; appears during rainy weather
DIET: omnivorous

APPEARANCE: Amefuri kozō resemble young boys. They wear children's kimonos, wooden clogs, and wide-brimmed straw hats or umbrellas on their heads. They are not particularly cute, and have pudgy, upturned noses.

BEHAVIOR: Despite their childish appearance, amefuri kozō are charged with the very important task of causing rainfall. Wherever they go, they cause clouds to form and rain to come down. In ancient China, amefuri kozō were thought to be the servants of the god of rainfall, who is known as Ushi in Japanese.

INTERACTIONS: Amefuri kozō are shy and rarely interact directly with people. However, they enjoy stealing people's umbrellas and wearing them as hats. They then cause rain showers to fall upon their victims.

ORIGIN: Amefuri kozō became widely known thanks to the printing boom during the Edo period. They were common characters in the cheap, pocket-sized publications sold by street vendors known as *kibyōshi*, or yellow covers. Kibyōshi were satirical comics, heavy on illustrations, depicting urban life with easy-to-read prose. Amefuri kozō and other priest boy yōkai became popular in these adult-oriented comic books. People enjoyed their grotesque, silly, yet somewhat cute appearance.

LEGENDS: Rain that falls while the sun is out is known in Japan as *kitsune no yomeiri*—fox weddings. Kitsune (fox yōkai) hold their weddings during sun showers. Before getting married, kitsune will say a prayer to the amefuri kozō for rain on their wedding day.

PRIEST BOY YŌKAI

There are many yōkai whose names end in kozō, a combination of 小 (*ko*; small) and 僧 (*sō*; priest or monk). This word literally means young Buddhist priests, but it can also be used as a general term for young boys. These kozō yōkai don't necessarily have any connection with religion, just like many *bōzu* and *nyūdō* yōkai aren't necessarily connected to Buddhism in any way.

Tōfu kozō 豆腐小僧

TRANSLATION: tofu priest boy
HABITAT: urban areas
DIET: omnivorous; loves tofu

APPEARANCE: Tōfu kozō are small yōkai who resemble human children except for their large heads and clawed fingers and toes. They wear little boys' kimonos and wide-brimmed hats—the typical outfit of tōfu-selling boys of the Edo period. They are usually depicted with two eyes, but in some illustrations they appear as having only one eye. They are usually found in urban areas in close proximity to people.

BEHAVIOR: Tōfu kozō are timid and weak yōkai. They are not known to be aggressive towards humans. On rare occasions, tofu kozō may follow people home on a rainy night. However, for the most part, they shy away from any confrontation.

INTERACTIONS: Tōfu kozō are first and foremost servant yōkai. Even among other yōkai, they are bullied and teased for their lack of strength. They get no respect; at most, they act as menial servants to more powerful yōkai.

ORIGIN: Tōfu kozō's origin is a mystery. Prior to the Edo period, there are no known stories about them. Some say that they are just one of many forms taken by an itachi, the shape-shifting weasel yōkai. Others say that tofu kozō are the offspring of a mikoshi nyūdō and a rokurokubi. Another possibility is that they are an invention of a creative artist looking to sell illustrated storybooks. Stories of tofu kozō first appeared in the penny-novels and pulp fiction of Edo in the 1770s. They became popular among the Edo upper class. These silly stories helped spawn the explosion of yōkai-related fiction that appeared in the latter half of the 18th century.

Tōfu kozō bears a strong resemblance to another yōkai called hitotsume kozō. The chief difference is that hitotsume kozō have only one eye and large tongues, while tofu kozō have two eyes and carry a plate of tofu. Both of these yōkai are weak, child-like creatures. They act as messengers to more powerful monsters. In some literature, the two yōkai are interchangeable. It has been suggested that tofu kozō may be closely related to, or may even have been copied from hitotsume kozō. However, there is not enough evidence either way to say for sure.

KATSURA OTOKO 桂男

TRANSLATION: katsura (the tree *Cercidiphyllum japonicum*) man
HABITAT: the moon
DIET: human life force

APPEARANCE: Katsura otoko is an incomparably beautiful man who lives in the face of the moon. He appears on moonlit nights and gazes back down at those who gaze up at him. His beauty is said to be so enchanting that people find it difficult to turn away—even to their own peril.

INTERACTIONS: If you gaze long enough at katsura otoko, he will extend his hand and beckon, calling you towards him. With each shake of his beckoning hand, your life span shrinks. If you stare long enough at katsura otoko, you may drop dead right on the spot!

ORIGIN: Katsura otoko originates in Chinese mythology. It is said there is a man who lives in a great palace on the moon. He spends his time pruning and chopping away at a gigantic katsura tree which grows there. As he prunes the tree, the shape of the moon grows smaller and less round until there is almost nothing left. Then the tree slowly grows its branches back—a just-so story to explain the waxing and waning of the moon.

SHIRIME 尻目

TRANSLATION: butt eye
ALTERNATE NAMES: nuppori bōzu
HABITAT: city streets, late at night
DIET: none; it just enjoys scaring people

APPEARANCE: From a distance, shirime appear to be normal human beings. When close enough, however, it becomes apparent that they are yōkai. Shirime have no facial features, but located in their buttholes are large eyes which shine like lightning.

BEHAVIOR: Shirime approach travelers on the road late at night, looking like men wearing a kimonos. Once they have your attention, they ask if you have a moment to spare. Before you can answer, the shirime drops its kimono to the ground and bends over, spreading its butt cheeks and revealing the giant, shining eye located inside of its butthole.

Other than this very startling behavior, shirime do not do anything harmful. They appear to thrive solely on the joy of scaring people.

ORIGIN: There are few documented encounters with shirime. Because of its alternate name (nuppori bōzu) and its shocking behavior, it is very likely that shirime are close relatives of the faceless nopperabō. In that case, a shirime's true form may simply be a shape-shifted animal playing a practical joke on humans.

Ōkaburo 大禿

TRANSLATION: big kamuro (an apprentice oiran)
ALTERNATE NAMES: ōkamuro
HABITAT: brothels
DIET: herbs and dew from chrysanthemums

APPEARANCE: Ōkaburo are cross-dressing yōkai found in brothels. They take the appearance of oversized *kamuro*, little girls employed as a servants in brothels. Only they are much larger than a typical girl of 5.

ORIGIN: The origins of this yōkai are vague. Ōkaburo are best known for their depiction by Toriyama Sekien. His ōkaburo is actually a male yōkai dressed up as a young kamuro, wearing a chrysanthemum-patterned kimono. His description makes an allusion to Peng Zu, a legendary Taoist wizard from China. Peng Zu lived past the age of 700 by having lots of sex with both women and men, and keeping a strict herbal diet which included licking the dew off of chrysanthemums. For this Peng Zu took the nickname Kiku-jidō, or chrysanthemum boy. Sekien likely intended his ōkaburo to be a pun referring to homosexual brothels in which young boys were dressed up as kamuro and offered to male patrons. Aside from the obvious connotations of having a young boy dressed up as a kamuro, the chrysanthemum was used as a secret symbol for homosexuality; the shape of the petals was supposed to represent an anus. The nickname chrysanthemum boy, the chrysanthemums on the kimono, and the image of licking the dew off of "chrysanthemums" leave little to the imagination as to what Sekien was alluding to with this yōkai.

A story of an ōkamuro with very different origins comes from a pleasure house in Hiroshima, where a particularly short-tempered oiran was employed. One day, her ohaguro (a tea-like mixture of hot water and iron filings used to blacken the teeth of courtesans) had been improperly prepared. The color would not stick to her teeth. Enraged, she grabbed the nearest kamuro and poured the entire pot of boiling liquid down the little girl's throat. The girl, vomiting up her insides, smeared her bloody handprints along the wall as she died in anguish. Ever since, it was said that the voice of that young kamuro could be heard at night, calling out for vengeance against the oiran.

PROSTITUTION IN OLD JAPAN: KAMURO AND OIRAN

The oldest profession has a long history in Japan, but the prostitution of the Edo period is perhaps the most widely romanticized and misunderstood. There is much confusion regarding the many types of entertainers found in old Japan, and the terms themselves have changed over the years. In the 16th century, walled "pleasure districts"—called *yukaku*—began to spring up in large cities. Eventually, these became the only areas in Japan where prostitution was legal; cities within cities specialized in the art of professional entertainment. The women employed in these neighborhoods were called *yujo*, or "pleasure girls." They were both prostitutes and entertainers.

Yujo had many ranks, but the highest and most elite were called *oiran*. Not simply prostitutes, oiran were highly trained and skilled entertainers. They were knowledgeable about many subjects, and seen as the epitome of beauty. Many developed celebrity status. To become an oiran, a woman had to undergo years of training. Young girls were sold to brothels at age 5. The training was lengthy; they would spend many years as a *kamuro*, acting as servants, messengers, and attendants for experienced oiran. If skillful and beautiful a kamuro could move up in rank to become an oiran herself.

Kejōrō 毛倡妓

TRANSLATION: hairy prostitute
HABITAT: brothels, red light districts
DIET: young, virile men

APPEARANCE: Kejōrō are prostitutes whose faces and bodies are hidden behind curtains of long, matted black hair. They appear in red-light districts and brothels. In most stories, only the hair on their heads is disturbingly thick and long, but in some stories, their whole bodies are covered in thick hair, like beasts.

BEHAVIOR: Despite their horrible appearance, kejōrō are said to be quite popular with other yōkai. In fact, male yōkai frequently fight each other over the kejōrō, competing for their affections. Kejōrō seem to return this devotion; in some stories, kejōrō cut off their hair and send it to their lovers—human or yōkai. Sometimes they tattoo their lover's name into their skin as a token of their undying love.

INTERACTIONS: Kejōrō's victims are young men who frequent brothels and red light districts. A man might think he sees a girl that he recognizes from behind, and run up to speak with her. When she turns around, her face and body are covered by a thick mat of hair that hides her features. The kejōrō shocks her victim in this way, which gives herself time to attack. She tangles him up in her hair and uses it to slice him up.

ORIGIN: The earliest records of kejōrō go back to Toriyama Sekien's *One Hundred Demons of the Past and Present*. There is some debate over his original description. Do kejōrō have a normal face under their mat of hair, or are they faceless monsters related to nopperabō and ohaguro bettari? Various yōkai researches weigh in on either side of the question.

MAIKO AND GEISHA

While kamuro and oiran were popular in the early Edo period, by the 19th century they had all but vanished. They were replaced by a new type of entertainer: the geisha. Geisha first appeared in the mid-18th century. They developed from the tradition of *odoriko*, dancing girls who performed as performers for hire but did not perform sexual services. Like oiran, geisha were highly trained and educated entertainers. Geisha appealed to a much broader class of people than the diva-like oiran did. Eventually, geisha grew so popular that they replaced oiran entirely. As with oiran, young girls began training to become geisha at age 5. They started as servants and gradually moved up in rank. At age 13, they could become maiko, or apprentice geisha. At the age of majority they could become fully-fledged geisha.

Despite the high class status of maiko and geisha in Japan, they are often mistakenly viewed as prostitutes overseas. Much of this misunderstanding comes from the occupation of Japan, when kimono-clad prostitutes dressed up as geisha appeared on the scene. These women primarily served American GIs, who did not know the difference between a "geisha girl" and real geisha. Eventually, "geisha girl" began to refer to any Japanese prostitute. This is why geisha have become so misunderstood in the West.

Iyaya 否哉

TRANSLATION: a slang expression meaning "No way!"
HABITAT: dark streets
DIET: as a human

APPEARANCE: From the back, iyaya look like attractive young women wearing beautiful clothing. When somebody calls out to them to get their attention, they turn around and reveal ugly, wrinkly faces like those of old men!

BEHAVIOR: Iyaya can be found anywhere. They prefer towns and roads at night where they are more likely to surprise lone travelers. They don't do anything harmful. Like many yōkai, they live just to shock people. That done, they wander off to find new victims.

Ōkubi 大首

TRANSLATION: giant head
HABITAT: hiding in large barns, or flying around in the sky
DIET: unknown

APPEARANCE: Ōkubi appear as enormous, severed heads, which fly through the sky. In most accounts they are female in appearance. Quite commonly they have blackened teeth.

INTERACTIONS: Ōkubi are little threat to humans. Their most common activity is to fly about harassing people: grinning at them, blowing away their umbrellas, or otherwise scaring them. According to some accounts, if an ōkubi breaths on any body part, that part will become inflamed. However, stories about serious injuries or deaths are rare to nonexistent.

LEGENDS: Eyewitness accounts of ōkubi were common during the Edo period. In a story from Inou Mononoke Roku, the protagonist Inou Heitarō opens the door to his storage house. He discovers that an enormous head of an old woman—the size of the entire storage house—has taken up residence inside. Curious, he pokes at the head with a long chopstick. Instead of bumping against the forehead of the ōkubi, the head is sticky and mushy and the chopstick slides right in.

Kasha 火車

TRANSLATION: fire cart
HABITAT: populated areas
DIET: fresh human corpses

APPEARANCE: Kasha are a type of bakeneko, or monster cat. They are bipedal felines as large as or larger than a human. Kasha are often accompanied by hellish flames or lightning. They appear during rain or stormy weather, and most often during the night. Their name sometimes causes them to be confused with other yōkai; kasha translates as "fire cart," but they do not use vehicles of any kind.

INTERACTIONS: Kasha, being bakeneko, often live among humans disguised as ordinary house cats or strays. However, they reveal their true forms during funeral services, when they leap down from rooftops to snatch corpses out of their coffins. Their motivations vary. Kasha are occasionally employed as messengers or servants of hell, in which case they are tasked with collecting the corpses of wicked humans to spirit off to hell for punishment. Other times, they steal corpses for their own uses—either to animate as puppets, or to eat.

It is nearly impossible to retrieve a person's remains after they have been snatched by a kasha. This makes passing on to the next life difficult. The best defense is to be prepared; temples in areas where kasha prowl have devised unique ways of defending against these monster cats. In Yamagata, clever priests hold two funeral ceremonies for the deceased. The first ceremony is a fake—the casket is filled only with rocks. If a kasha comes for the body it will end up with nothing. The real ceremony takes place afterwards, when the risk of a kasha encounter is lessened. In Ehime Prefecture (old Iyo Province), a head shaving razor may be placed on top of the coffin as a ward against kasha. In Miyazaki (old Hyūga Province), priests chant *"kasha ni wa kuwasen (don't be eaten by a kasha)"* two times in front of the funeral procession. In Okayama Prefecture (old Bitchū, Bizen and Mimasaka Provinces), priests play a *myōhachi*—a type of cymbal used in religious ceremonies—in order to keep kasha away.

ORIGIN: Kasha were once ordinary house cats. Like other animals in Japanese folklore, as cats age their tails grow longer, and they begin to develop magical powers. Some turn into bakeneko. More powerful cats turn into nekomata. Beyond that some turn into kasha. Fear of such demonic cats has long existed in Japan. Since ancient times, folk wisdom tells us, "Don't let cats near dead bodies," and, "If a cat jumps over the coffin, the corpse inside the coffin will rise." Fears such as these have given rise to superstitious traditions such as cutting a cat's tail short in order to prevent it from learning magic.

WHERE'S THE CART?

Kasha have a quirky name: it means fire cart, but there is no cart! The original reading of this yōkai's kanji is hi no kuruma, and it does actually refer to a corpse-stealing demon pulling a flaming cart. The demon who pulls the hi no kuruma is a kind of mōryō that carries the dead off to hell to be tortured. When the name kasha was written down in kanji, the characters for hi no kuruma were used for their phonetic value and because of the kasha's corpse-stealing tendencies. The kanji for mōryō have also been used as an ateji (choosing kanji for meaning only, without regard to the reading) to write "kasha," as mōryō is also general term for corpse-stealing yōkai.

HONE KARAKASA 骨傘

TRANSLATION: skeletal umbrella
HABITAT: anywhere humans live
DIET: none

APPEARANCE: Hone karakasa are tsukumogami born from tattered and torn up old Chinese-style paper umbrellas which have lost their covering. Only the "bones" remain. They dance through the sky like wild birds. Hone karakasa are closely related to other umbrella tsukumogami, such as the karakasa kozō.

Nurikabe 塗壁

TRANSLATION: painted wall
HABITAT: coastal areas; encountered on dark streets and alleys
DIET: unknown

APPEARANCE: Because these yōkai are usually said to be invisible, little is known about the true form of nurikabe. During the Edo period, however, artists began to illustrate this creature. They gave it an appearance somewhere between a grotesque, fantastic beast and a flat, white wall. Modern representations of the nurikabe depict it as a plain, gray, bipedal wall with vague facial features.

BEHAVIOR: Nurikabe appear mysteriously on roads late at night. As you are walking, an enormous, invisible wall materializes right before your eyes and blocks your way. There is no way to slip around this yōkai; nurikabe extend as far as to the left and right as you might try to go. There is no way over them, nor can they be knocked down. However, it is said that if you tap a nurikabe near the ground with a stick, it will vanish and allow you to continue on your way.

ORIGIN: The true nature of the nurikabe is surrounded in mystery. Based on its name, it seems to be related to other household spirits known as tsukumogami. It has also been suggested that nurikabe are simply another manifestation of shape-shifting itachi (weasel) or tanuki. Mischievous tanuki are said to enlarge their magical scrotums into an invisible wall in order to play pranks on unsuspecting humans.

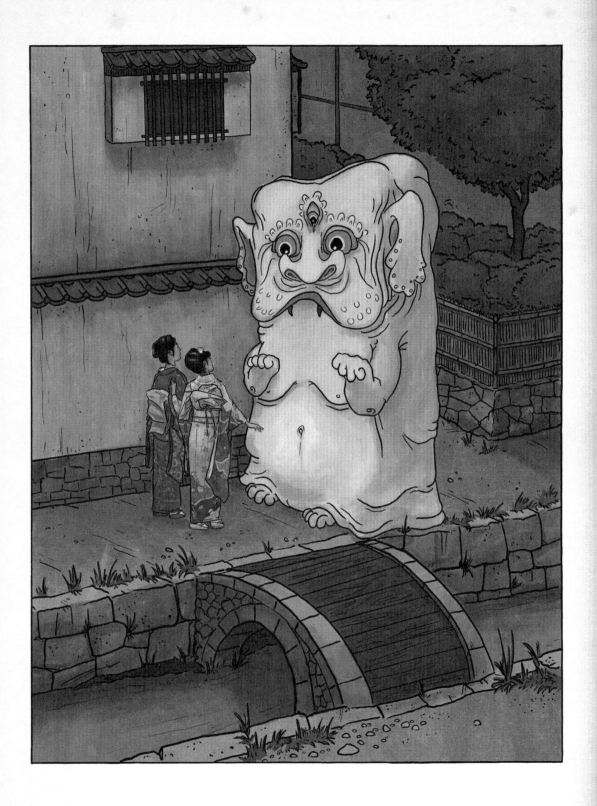

Sōgenbi 叢原火

TRANSLATION: Sōgen's fire
HABITAT: spotted at Mibu-dera in Kyōto
DIET: none

APPEARANCE: Sōgenbi is a type of hi no tama, or fireball yōkai. It appears as the anguished head of an old monk, covered in flame, and flies about the sky.

LEGENDS: Long ago, at the temple of Mibu-dera in southern Kyōto there lived a monk named Sōgen. Sōgen was a wicked monk. He would steal money out of the temple's saisenbako, a large wooden box which holds offerings. He also made off with precious oil, which was to be used as an offering for the gods. Sōgen sold it in secret, keeping the money for himself. This went on for many years, until he eventually grew old and died. Because of his wickedness, Sōgen was reborn as a yōkai. Shortly after his death, it was said that the flaming head of old Sōgen could be seen floating about in the vicinity of Mibu-dera.

HAKA NO HI 墓の火

TRANSLATION: grave fire
HABITAT: tombs, graveyards, and burial grounds
DIET: none

APPEARANCE: Haka no hi are mysterious, supernatural fires, or kaika. They spout forth from the base of graves.

ORIGIN: The cause of haka no hi is unknown. It is commonly believed to be a result of failure on the part of the grave's owner to reach enlightenment and pass on to Nirvana. The flames are thought to be residual energy from worldly attachments, or else feelings of grudge or resentment, coming from the remains interred in the grave.

Oitekebori 置行堀

TRANSLATION: "drop-it-and-get-out-of-here" canal

APPEARANCE: Oitekebori is a mysterious apparition that was seen in Honjo, part of Sumida ward in present-day Tōkyō. It takes the form of a human ghost, and haunts fishermen and others who stray too close to its home in the canals. The oitekebori name derives from a slang version of the phrase, "*oite ike!*" meaning, "drop it and get out of here!"

ORIGIN: Nobody really knows exactly what the oitekebori is. The most likely explanation is a kappa. Hungry and too lazy to fish on his own, it terrorized innocent fishermen and stole their catches. Other explanations blame a tricky tanuki. Still other explanations exist, covering everything from a yūrei, a kawauso, a mujina, or a suppon—a soft-shelled turtle-turned-yōkai.

LEGENDS: Long ago, Honjo was full of canals and waterways teaming with fish. It was common for people to make their livings catching and selling fish caught in the moat system.

One night, two fishermen were fishing in a particular spot in Honjo at sunset. They noticed that they were catching more fish than usual. So they fished and fished, filling their baskets to the brim. After some time, when they could hold no more fish, they happily packed up their tackle and prepared to carry their large catches home. Just as they were about to leave, they heard an eerie, terrible voice come up from the canal. It shouted "oiteke!"

What happens next depends on who is telling the story. Some say that both fishermen dropped their baskets and fled; when they returned to the canals later that night, both baskets were empty. Others say that they fled home with their baskets, but when they got home there wasn't a single fish in the baskets. But the most chilling version goes like this:

Both fisherman turned and fled from the canal. One of them dropped his basket and the other took his basket with him. The fisherman who dropped his basket ran all the way back to his house and bolted the door shut. The other fisherman didn't get very far—a ghostly hand rose up out of the canal and dragged him down into the water, basket and all. He was never seen again.

NUE 鵺

TRANSLATION: none; the characters connote night and bird
HABITAT: unknown; only seen in the sky, accompanied by black clouds
DIET: unknown

APPEARANCE: The nue is one of the oldest yōkai recorded, first appearing in the Kojiki (712 CE), an account of the early histories of Japan. It also appeared in the Heian-period encyclopedia *Wamyo Ruijusho* (938 CE), and again in the *Heike Monogatari* (1371 CE), a record of one of Japan's bloodiest civil wars and most tragic family clans. The nue has the head of a monkey, the body of a tanuki, the tail of a snake, and the limbs of a tiger. In ancient times, it was thought to be a kind of nocturnal bird—its call was supposed to sound like that of a White's thrush. Thus, its name is written with a kanji that contains the meanings "night" and "bird."

BEHAVIOR: Little is known about the nue's natural habitat and lifestyle. While sightings throughout history have been rare, nue are considered to be evil monsters. The few times that humans and nue have crossed paths, the results have been disastrous.

LEGENDS: One famous nue attack occurred in the summer of 1153 in Kyōto. Emperor Konoe had nightmares every night, and grew terribly ill. Neither medicine nor prayers had any effect, and the illness was attributed to some evil spirit visiting the palace early in the morning. These events climaxed days later in a storm, which appeared over the imperial palace around 2 AM. Lightning struck the roof, setting it on fire. The emperor summoned the legendary samurai Minamoto no Yorimasa. To deal with the evil spirit, Yorimasa brought his legendary bow which he received from Minamoto no Yorimitsu, and his trusted companion I no Hayata. During the night, a strange wind blew over them, followed by a black cloud. Yorimasa fired an arrow into the clouds above the palace. Out from the sky came a horrible scream as a nue dropped to the earth. I no Hayata leaped upon the body, dealing it the finishing blow. The emperor immediately recovered from his illness, and rewarded the heroes with the legendary katana Shishiō for their service. This event has been immortalized in numerous paintings and ukiyoe prints.

After the nue was slain, the inhabitants of Kyōto were afraid of a retaliatory curse for killing the beast. They loaded its body in a ship and sent it down the Kamo River. The boat with the nue's corpse eventually washed up on the shore near the village of Ashiya, in Settsu Province. The good citizens of Ashiya removed the nue's body, built it a burial mound, and gave it a proper funeral. You can still visit the mound today, known as Nuezuka.

Itsumade 以津真天

Translation: "until when?"
Alternate names: itsumaden
Diet: the lamentation of the dead

Appearance: Itsumade are kaichō, or strange birds. They have the face of a human with a pointed beak, and the body of a snake with wings, and terrible claws. Their wingspan is 4.8 meters.

Behavior: Itsumade appear in the night sky during times of trouble—such as plagues and disasters, or flying over battlegrounds where many have died. In particular, they fly over places where there is suffering or death, yet little has been done to alleviate the pain of the living or pacify the spirits of the dead. The strange birds fly about in circles all night long, crying out in a terrible voice.

Origin: Itsumade make their first recorded appearance in the *Taiheiki*, a fictional history of Japan written in the 14th century. According to the *Taiheiki*, a terrible plague spread during the fall of 1334. The suffering of the plague victims is what summoned the itsumade.

Itsumade's name is not written in the *Taiheiki*; it was added later by Toriyama Sekien. He named this yōkai for its horrible cry of "Itsumademo?" which means, "Until when?" The birds appear to be asking those below how long will this suffering go unnoticed. It is thought that the spirits of the dead and suffering form into onryō which take the shape of these birds. They demand recognition of their suffering and torment.

Legends: One night during the fall of 1334, the itsumade suddenly appeared above the hall for state ceremonies, crying out, "Itsumademo? Itsumademo?" Panic erupted amongst the people of the capital. The same creature came back the next night, and every night thereafter. Finally, the imperial court decided that something had to be done. They recalled Minamoto no Yorimasa's triumph against the nue many years earlier, and decided to summon the warrior Oki no Jirouzaemon Hiroari. Hiroari was an expert archer. He used a signal arrow that let off a loud whistle as it flew, and shot the monster out of the sky. Afterwards, Hiroari was given the name Mayumi, meaning true bow.

Mayumi Hiroari went on to become a famous warrior, and settled down in Chikugo Province in what is now Miyama City, Fukuoka Prefecture. His grave still stands there. The area was renamed in his honor after he died.

ONMORAKI 陰摩羅鬼

TRANSLATION: shadowy unpious demon
HABITAT: temples and places where people have recently died
DIET: impiety

APPEARANCE: Onmoraki are bird-like monsters with black feathers, bright eyes that shine like lanterns, and a ghastly human face. They are skilled mimics, and shake their feathers as they give off their shrill, terrifying call.

INTERACTIONS: Onmoraki appear near temples, particularly in the presence of neglectful priests. They sneak up on sleeping priests and surprise them, scolding them in a perfect imitation of their own voices. When the priest wakes up and flees in terror, the onmoraki vanishes into the shadows.

ORIGIN: Onmoraki come from the bodies of the recently deceased. When people die but do not receive enough memorial prayer, their life energy can transform into this grotesque, bird-like demon. The name onmoraki comes from a play on words emphasizing demonic interference with achieving Buddhist enlightenment. The first part of the name, *on*, comes from onmyō, the Japanese word for yin and yang. On represents yin, the shadow, the unseen, and hidden, secret things—in this case it refers to demons which live in the shadows and in the hidden parts of the world. The second part of the name, *mora*, refers to Mara, a Buddhist demon who personifies unskillfulness, impiety, and the death of the spirit—a reference to the poor quality of memorial services which cause this yōkai to come forth. The last part of the name, *ki*, simply means demon—emphasizing the fact that this monster truly is a demon.

Waniguchi 鰐口

Translation: alligator mouth; shrine bell

Appearance: Waniguchi are tsukumogami which come from the circular, hollow bells found at shrine entrances. These bells are rung when praying to the shrine's gods. When one of these bells becomes a yōkai, it sprouts a reptilian body and tail. The bell becomes the creature's head, opening and closing like an alligator's mouth.

Origin: The bells at shrines are called waniguchi due to the wide split along the bottom rim. This gives them the distinct look of an alligator's mouth. This yōkai first appeared in tsukumogami picture scrolls as a pun based off of the word for shrine bell.

Nyūnai suzume 入内雀

TRANSLATION: imperial palace-penetrating sparrow
ALTERNATE NAMES: sanekata suzume (Sanekata sparrow)
HABITAT: the imperial palace of ancient Kyōto
DIET: all of the emperor's breakfast

APPEARANCE: Nyūnai suzume has the appearance of an ordinary russet sparrow, but in reality it is the ghost of an imperial attendant named Fujiwara no Sanekata.

LEGENDS: During the reign of Emperor Ichijō (960-1011 CE) lived a nobleman named Fujiwara no Sanekata. One day, he got into a quarrel over some gossip started by Fujiwara no Yukinari. In a rage, Sanekata snatched Yukinari's hat and threw it away. For his bad temper, Sanekata was demoted and exiled to a solitary island in Mutsu Province in the northeast. Sanekata nursed his resentment towards those back in the court at Kyōto. Three years into his exile, he died, with thoughts of vengeance poisoning his heart.

When the news of Sanekata's death reached Kyōto, a strange event began. Every morning, when the servants placed food out for the imperial court to eat at the Seiryōden palace, a phantom sparrow would swoop in, gobble up all of the food in an instant, and flew off. No matter how much food was laid out, the sparrow devoured every grain of rice. It left nothing for the palace inhabitants.

It was not long before the court grew scared of this bird. Not content with just eating the court's feasts, it destroyed all of the crops in the fields. Nobody knew how to stop the sparrow's attacks. Rumors spread that the sparrow could only be the vengeful ghost—or onryō—of Fujiwara no Sanekata.

At the same time, Saint Kanshi, the high priest of Kangaku-in, had a sparrow visit him in a dream. The sparrow identified itself as the spirit of Sanekata. He desperately longed to return to his beloved Kyōto, and asked the priest to chant and pray for him. The next morning, Kanshi discovered the body of a single sparrow lying dead at the base of a tree on the temple grounds. He recognized the sparrow as the transformed spirit of Fujiwara no Sanekata, and built a small grave. Kanshi mourned it and prayed for its soul.

After the sparrow's grave was built, the attacks stopped. Years later, Kangaku-in's name changed to Kyōjaku-ji, or Sparrow Temple. While Kyōto has changed dramatically since that time, the little grave where the sparrow was buried still remains.

Fujiwara no Sanekata's legacy lives in another way: the common Japanese name for the russet sparrow is nyūnai suzume.

TERATSUTSUKI 寺つつき

TRANSLATION: templepecker (as opposed to woodpecker)
HABITAT: Buddhist temples
DIET: its own rage

APPEARANCE: Teratsutsuki is the onryō of Mononobe no Moriya, who lived in the 6th century CE. His onryō took the form of a ghostly woodpecker that tried to destroy Hōryū-ji and Shitennō-ji temples, until it was driven away by Prince Shōtoku.

LEGENDS: Long, long ago, when Japan was still called Yamato and the capital was located in Yamato Province, the nobility was divided into two kabane, or political groups: shinbetsu and kōbetsu. The shinbetsu clans claimed to be descended from the gods, and the kōbetsu clans claimed to be descended from the imperial family. The highest ranking titles in these groups were muraji, for the shinbetsu, and omi, for the kōbetsu. Their rivalry flamed in the 6th century CE, when Buddhism to was introduced to Yamato from China.

Mononobe no Moriya was the leader of the Mononobe clan and a muraji. As a shinbetsu clan with ties to Japan's native gods, the Mononobe supported the old Shinto religion. Moriya's rival was Soga no Umako. As an omi, Umako supported the promotion of Buddhism throughout Yamato. Moriya and Umako both had considerable influence in the imperial court, although Moriya held the higher favor during the reign of Emperor Bidatsu (572-585). But when Emperor Yōmei, a Buddhist, took power in 585, Umako rose in power.

Emperor Yōmei died two years later in 587. Both the Mononobe clan and Soga clan tried to influence the succession of the imperial title. They each supported a different prince, and fought bitterly for their clans' interests. Finally, war broke out. During the war, Mononobe no Moriya sought to purge the foreign religion from his homeland. He set fire to Buddhist temples and tossed statues of Buddha into canals—including the first such statues brought to Yamato. Moriya and Umako mustered their armies and met on the battlefield in Kawachi Province. There, at the Battle of Mount Shigi, Mononobe no Moriya was killed by Soga no Umako and Prince Shōtoku. The Mononobe clan was almost completely exterminated. Afterwards, the Soga clan rose to even higher prominence. Prince Shōtoku, a devout Buddhist, began the construction of many new Buddhist temples.

The spirit of defeated Mononobe no Moriya did not rest. As he lay dying, he was filled with hatred and resentment, and transformed into an onryō. Moriya's ghost took the form of a ghostly woodpecker—the teratsutsuki—which would be seen at the temples built by Prince Shōtoku. The phantom bird pecked furiously at the wooden buildings, determined even in death to destroy the heretical new religion. Prince Shōtoku finally drove away the teratsutsuki by transforming into a hawk and attacking it. After that, the ghost of Mononobe no Moriya was never seen again.

GAGOZE 元興寺

TRANSLATION: none; named for the temple which he haunted
ALTERNATE NAMES: gangōji no oni, gagoji, guwagoze, gangō, gango
DIET: children

APPEARANCE: Gagoze is a *reiki*, or demon ghost, who haunted the temple Gangō-ji many centuries ago. He appears as a hideous demon dressed in monks robes, crawling about on all fours. His legend is preserved at Gangō-ji, which was founded in 593 by Soga no Umako.

LEGENDS: Long ago in Owari Province, during the time of Emperor Bidatsu, a thunder god fell out of the sky in bolt of lightning. A peasant investigated the spot where the bolt struck, and discovered the thunder god in the form of a young boy. The peasant raised his cane with the intention to kill the creature, but the god pleaded to spare his life. The thunder god promised to give the peasant and his wife a young boy as strong as a god if the peasant would help him. The peasant agreed, and helped the thunder god to build a boat which allowed him to return to heaven.

Shortly after, the peasant and his wife had a child. Just as promised the child was as strong as a thunder god. As the boy grew, he became renowned far and wide for his superhuman strength. By the time he turned 10, he had grown so powerful and boastful that he challenged a prince to a contest of strength and won. This attracted attention of the imperial court, and the boy was apprenticed to Gangō-ji.

Shortly after he joined Gangō-ji, the temple's young apprentices began dying strange deaths one by one. Every morning, the fresh corpse of one of the boys would be found by the temple's bell tower. The monks decided that an evil spirit was infiltrating the temple at night and committing the murders. The peasant's son resolved to solve the mystery. He volunteered to catch whatever was killing the boys.

That night, the boy placed covered lanterns in the four corners of the bell tower. He instructed an older monk to wait by the lanterns and uncover them once he grabbed the evil spirit. The boy waited by the bell tower. At midnight a hunched creature came crawling towards the tower. It saw the boy, however, and ran away.

A few hours later, hunger got the better of the creature and it slinked back. The boy sprang and caught it by the hair, but the monk was too scared to uncover the lanterns. Summoning his superhuman strength, the boy dragged the creature to each corner of the tower and uncovered the lights. In the lamplight, he could see that the creature was a reiki—the ghost of an oni.

The reiki pulled back so hard that it ripped off its own scalp. Once free, it scampered away into the darkness, leaving its hair in the boy's hand. When morning came, the priests followed the bloody trail left by the creature. They found the grave of a lazy, wicked servant formerly employed by the temple. The servant's spirit had transformed into the demon ghost that was responsible for the murders.

After that, the reiki never returned to the temple again. The monster's scalp became one of the holy treasures of Gangō-ji. The boy became famous far and wide. He used his superhuman strength to irrigate the temple's fields, and eventually took the name Dōjō and became a splendid priest. After he died, he was enshrined as one of the gods of Gangō-ji.

SHUTEN DŌJI 酒呑童子

TRANSLATION: a nickname meaning "little drunkard"

APPEARANCE: Shuten dōji is an oni—a great, red-skinned, horned demon with superhuman strength and a wicked, corrupt heart. He is considered to be the king of the oni. Along with the ghost of Emperor Sutoku and the nine-tailed kitsune Tamamo no Mae, he is one of the Three Terrible Yōkai of Japan

LEGENDS: Shuten dōji was not born an oni. There are many stories about how he came to be, but most of them say that he was originally a human boy born over a thousand years ago, either in Ōmi or Etchū Province. His mother was a human woman and his father was the great dragon Yamata no Orochi. How he changed from boy to demon varies greatly from story to story, but the one popular version goes like this: There was a young boy who was supernaturally strong and abnormally intelligent for his age. Everyone around him constantly called him a demon child due to his incredible strength and wit. He gradually became anti-social and resentful of others. At age six even his own mother abandoned him. Orphaned, the boy became an apprentice priest at Mt. Hiei in Kyōto. Naturally, he was the strongest and smartest of the young acolytes. But he grew resentful of them as well. He slacked off on his studies and got into fights. He also fell into drinking, which was forbidden to monks. He could out-drink anyone and everyone who was willing to sit down and drink against him. Because of his fondness for alcohol, he became known as Shuten dōji, "the little drunkard."

One night there was a festival at the temple, and Shuten dōji showed up very drunk. He put on an oni mask and went around playing pranks on his fellow priests, jumping out from the darkness to scare them and such. At the end of the night, he tried to take off his mask but found he couldn't—to his horror, it had fused to his body! Ashamed, scared, and scolded by his masters for being drunk, he fled into the mountains where he would no longer have to interact with other humans. He saw them as weak, foolish, and hypocritical. He lived there on the outskirts of Kyōto for many years, stealing food and alcohol from villagers, and drinking vast quantities of alcohol. His banditry eventually attracted groups of thieves and criminals, who stuck with him loyally and became the foundation for his gang.

Living in exile, Shuten dōji grew in power and knowledge. He mastered strange, dark magic, and taught it to his thugs. He met another demon child like him, named Ibaraki dōji, who became his chief servant. Over time, the young man and his gang transformed into oni. Eventually, he had an entire clan of oni and yōkai thugs who prowled the highways, terrorizing the people of Kyōto. He and his gang eventually settled on Mount Ōe. In a dark castle, he plotted to conquer the capital and rule as emperor.

Shuten dōji and his gang rampaged through Kyōto, capturing noble virgins, drinking their blood and eating their organs raw. Finally, a band of heroes led by the legendary warrior Minamoto no Yorimitsu assaulted Shuten dōji's palace. With the help of some magical poison, they were able to assault the oni band during a bout of heavy drinking. They cut off the drunken Shuten dōji's head, but even after cutting it off, the head continued to bite at Minamoto no Yorimitsu.

Because the head belonged to an oni and was unholy, they buried it outside of the city limits, at a mountain pass called Oinosaka. The cup and bottle of poison that Minamoto no Yorimitsu used are said to be kept at the temple Nariai-ji in Kyōto.

IBARAKI DŌJI 茨木童子

TRANSLATION: a nickname meaning "thorn tree child"

APPEARANCE: Ibaraki dōji is one of the most famous and most feared demons to have wreaked havoc upon Japan. She was the chief deputy to Shuten dōji, the greatest oni of all.

ORIGIN: Not very much is known about Ibaraki dōji's life. It isn't really even known if Ibaraki dōji was male or female. Most stories and illustrations depict Ibaraki dōji as a kijo, or a female oni. Yet there are other stories which refer to Shuten dōji's deputy as a male. There is also a rumor that she and Shuten dōji were not only partners in crime, but also lovers. What is known is that Ibaraki dōji was a wholly terrible and fearsome monster. It was bent on doing as much damage in the human world as possible.

LEGENDS: Ibaraki dōji's most famous story takes place at Rashōmon, the southern gate of old Kyōto's city walls. Rashōmon was built in 789, but after the Heian period it fell into serious disrepair. It was overgrown and unkempt, an unsavory place. Thieves and bandits hung out near it. It even served as a dumping point for unwanted babies, and a spot to dispose of murder victims. But the scariest part of its haunted reputation was the legend of Rashōmon no oni—the demon of Rashōmon.

After his celebrated victory over Shuten dōji, the hero Minamoto no Yorimitsu returned triumphant to Kyōto. He was celebrating at his home with his deputies—Sakata no Kintoki, Urabe no Suetake, Usui Sadamitsu, and Watanabe no Tsuna—when the noble Fujiwara no Yasumasa informed them that an oni was seen haunting Rashōmon gate. Watanabe no Tsuna, had just returned from a great battle with Shuten dōji's clan; he could not believe there were any oni left. Single-handedly, he went out to investigate. He mounted his horse and traveled south.

When Tsuna arrived at the gate, a great howling wind broke out and his horse could travel no further. He dismounted and went on foot. Approaching the gate in the fierce gale, he noticed an enormous hand reach out of the dark to grab his helmet. Tsuna wasted no time, and swung his great katana around. He severed the arm of an enormous demon—it was Ibaraki dōji, coming to avenge the murder of Shuten dōji. The injured demon ran away, leaving her arm behind. Rashōmon was no longer haunted.

Ibaraki dōji later returned to Rashōmon, looking for her arm. She disguised herself as Watanabe no Tsuna's wet-nurse, and was able to steal back her severed arm and flee. After that, her whereabouts were never known again. Though for many years after, in some town or another, villagers would claim that they had seen Ibaraki dōji coming or going. The monster always appeared in connection with some kind of mischief.

Hashihime 橋姫

TRANSLATION: princess of the bridge
HABITAT: very old, very long bridges

DIET: rage and jealousy

APPEARANCE: Hashihime are spirits who inhabit bridges—in particular, very old and very long bridges. Hashihime often take different forms depending on the occasion. However, they are most commonly depicted wearing white robes, white face-paint, and crowned with an iron trivet lit with five candles. This is a ceremonial outfit used to perform curses.

INTERACTIONS: Hashihime ferociously guard the bridges they inhabit. As with most spirits connected to a location, they are competitive and jealous. If you praise or speak positively about another bridge while on top of a hashihime's bridge, or if you recite lines from certain noh plays that feature a woman's wrath as the main theme, something terrible is likely to happen.

Despite their fearsome nature, hashihime are highly honored by the people who live nearby the bridges they inhabit. Shrines are established in their honor. In times of war, residents beseech their local hashihime to guard the bridge against invaders. In times of peace, hashihime are revered as goddesses of separation and severing. They are asked to aid people in things such as break-ups, divorce, and severing bad luck. So strong is their power of severing that it is considered taboo for lovers or wedding processions to pass in front of a hashihime shrine together. If newlyweds need to cross a bridge inhabited by a hashihime, they must instead pass underneath it on a boat or risk cursing their marriage.

LEGENDS: The most famous hashihime story comes from *Tsurugi no Maki*, in *The Tale of the Heike* and is retold in the noh play *Kanawa*. A woman visited the Kifune-jinja in Kyōto at the hour of the ox (roughly 2 am). She was filled with rage and jealousy towards her ex-husband who had thrown her away for another woman. Night after night she visited the shrine, praying to the gods enshrined there to turn her into a powerful demon. The woman wanted nothing else other than to see her ex-husband destroyed, even at the cost of her own life. After seven nights of pilgrimage, her prayers were answered—the gods told her that if she immersed herself in the Uji River for twenty-one nights, she would become a living demon.

The woman did as she was bid. She donned a white robe and tied her hair up into five horns. She painted her face and covered her body in crimson dye. She placed an upturned trivet on her head and attached torches to each foot of the iron stand. She lit a torch on both ends and placed it in her mouth. She immersed herself in the Uji River, and for twenty-one days she kindled the hatred in her heart. Just as the gods told her, she transformed into a terrible kijo with supreme power. She had become the hashihime of Uji.

That night, her ex-husband awoke from a horrible dream with a premonition of danger. He sought out the famous onmyōji, Abe no Seimei, who recognized the dream as a sign that the man's former wife would come and destroy the couple that very night. Seimei promised to save them. He went to their house, recited magical prayers, and crafted two katashiro—magical paper doll representations of the man and his new wife. These were meant to be used as substitutionary targets for the hashihime's rage. That night, as Seimei had predicted, the demon appeared. Seimei's magic worked; the hashihime attacked the two katashiro instead of the real couple. Her power was reflected back upon her and she was driven away. The demon, realizing that she could not overcome Abe no Seimei's magic, promised that she would return another time and vanished.

Hannya 般若

TRANSLATION: wisdom; specifically the Buddhist concept of Perfect Wisdom

APPEARANCE: Hannya refers to demons or oni; more specifically to female demons called kijo—even more specifically to those kijo which appear in noh theater. They were once human women who were consumed by jealousy and transformed into demonesses. The name hannya also refers to a specific type of demon mask used in noh theater.

There are three grades of hannya: namanari, chūnari, and honnari. Namanari hannya are kijo that still resemble human women. They have small horns and use dark magic to perform their evil deeds, such as summoning ikiryō to attack their enemies. They are not completely evil; there remains a chance for these beginner demons to return to humanity. Chūnari hannya are mid-level demons. They have long, sharp horns, tusk-like fangs, and more powerful magic. However, they are still vulnerable to Buddhist prayers. Honnari hannya are true demons and the most powerful of the three. They have serpentine bodies and breathe fire. Honnari hannya have embraced their jealousy so deeply that there is no calming their fury.

ORIGIN: Hannya originate from the Sanskrit term for wisdom—specifically *Prajñāpāramitā*, the highest form of Buddhist wisdom which leads to enlightenment. The juxtaposition of the highest form of wisdom and creatures who represent direct opposition to that wisdom comes from the use of the hannya mask in noh. In the play Aoi no Ue, a shugenja (an ascetic mystic) exorcises the spirit of the hannya Lady Rokujō from Lady Aoi. As it is driven away, the evil spirit cries out, "Oh, how horrible! The voice of wisdom is like a demon!" Since then, demon masks and wisdom have been associated with each other.

The three most famous hannya from Japanese literature are Lady Rokujō from *Aoi no Ue*, Kurozuka from *Kurozuka*, and Kiyo hime from *Dōjō-ji*.

KUROZUKA 黒塚

TRANSLATION: Black Mounds; named for the area she haunted
ALTERNATE NAMES: Adachigahara no Onibaba (The Demon Hag of Adachigahara)

APPEARANCE: Kurozuka is one of the most well-known kijo, or demon women, in Japanese folklore. She is a popular subject in the arts, starring in everything from paintings to ukiyoe prints to noh plays. She has gone by many names. The most famous is *Kurozuka*, or the Witch of the Black Mounds, but she is also known as the Demon Hag of Adachigahara, or even just simply Onibaba—the Demon Hag.

LEGENDS: Kurozuka's story has changed over the years and through various adaptations. A popular version of her story goes like this:

Long ago, a wealthy noble couple had a daughter whom they loved very much. She was sickly, however, and by the age of five she had never spoken a word. The worried couple consulted with priests and doctors. Finally, a doctor told them that the only way to cure their daughter was to feed her a fresh liver from an unborn fetus.

The couple summoned their daughter's nanny and gave her the task of obtaining the liver. Expecting that it would take some time to find someone willing to give up their baby's liver, the nanny prepared for a long journey. She gave the daughter a protection charm and promised not to return empty-handed. Then she left.

The nanny traveled for days, months, and eventually years without finding any family willing to give up their baby's life. Eventually, her travels brought her to the moors of Adachigahara, in Fukushima. Despondent, she decided that if nobody would give her a liver, she would have to take one. She made camp in a cave off of the road and decided to wait for a pregnant woman to pass by.

Many more years passed. Finally, a lone pregnant woman came walking by on the road. The nanny leaped out of the cave and slew the traveler with her knife. She carved the pregnant woman's belly open, killing the fetus, and harvested its fresh liver. Only after the deed was done did the nanny look down at her victim. She noticed the young woman was wearing an old but familiar protection charm—the same one that she had given the daughter so many years ago. The knowledge of what she had done weighed so heavily on her that the nanny went insane. She transformed into a hannya.

The Demon Hag of Adachigahara, as she came to be known, developed fearsome magical powers. She lured travelers into her shelter and invited them to spend the night. After which she murdered them in their sleep. She remained on the moors of Adachigahara for many years, murdering any lone travelers who passed by her cave and eating their remains.

In the noh version of her story, the demon woman is eventually visited by traveling Buddhist priests whom she plans to kill. While she is out gathering firewood, the priests find a room full of dead bodies and bones. They recognize her as the Demon of Adachigahara. She chases after them, but they are able to hold her back with their Buddhist prayers. They manage to drive the evil spirit from her and banish it forever. When the demon spirit is driven from her body, the nanny reverts to being an old woman and dies. The monks bury her remains and build a grave among the black mounds that she haunted.

MOMIJI 紅葉

TRANSLATION: literally "maple leaves;" used as a name

ALTERNATE NAMES: Sarashina hime (Princess Sarashina)

APPEARANCE: Momiji is a famous kijo and an example of a hannya—a woman who has transformed into a powerful demon. Her tale is famous in Japanese theater. The noh play *Momijigari* ("Fall-Leaf Hunting" or "Hunting Momiji") first appeared hundreds of years ago during the Muromachi period. During the Meiji period it was remade as a kabuki play. *Momijigari* was made into a film in 1899, becoming one of the first Japanese films. It was designated an Important Cultural Property in 2009.

LEGENDS: Long ago, a powerful witch named Momiji lived in the mountains of Shinano Province. Her story takes place during the season of fall-leaf-viewing, when groups of people gathered in the mountains for festivals and parties under the falling red, orange, and gold leaves.

During this time, a samurai named Taira no Koremochi was charged by a local Hachiman shrine with hunting oni. His hunt had taken him to Togakushi Mountain, where a particularly nasty kijo was said to live.

Koremochi and his retainers climbed the beautiful mountain and came upon a small group of aristocrats having a leaf-viewing party. Koremochi sent one of his retainers ahead to investigate. The retainer approached to inquire about the party. He was told that a noble princess was hosting it; however, the ladies in waiting would not tell him the princess's name. Just as Koremochi and his retainers decided to continue on their mission, one of the ladies-in-waiting approached and told them that her mistress had heard of Koremochi before. She wanted to invite them to her party. Despite his mission, Koremochi could not turn down an offer from a princess. He and his companions agreed.

At the party, the warriors were introduced to an extremely beautiful young woman named Princess Sarashina. They sat and enjoyed watching the leaves, drinking sake, and dancing. Koremochi asked the princess if she would dance for him, and she did. Soon the men became drunk and sleepy and dozed off under the beautiful trees.

As he slept, Koremochi dreamed of Hachiman and his mission. The god told him that Princess Sarashina was actually the kijo Momiji in disguise, and that he must kill her with the holy katana, Kogarasumaru ("Little Crow"). When Koremochi woke up, the sword he dreamed of was in his hand—a gift from Hachiman. He knew that the dream had been real. He chased after the women, when suddenly a huge firestorm broke out. Flame and wind lit up the mountain. Suddenly, a ten foot tall hannya with horns made of burning trees appeared. An intense battle raged between the samurai and the demoness. In the end Koremochi slew the Witch of Togakushi Mountain thanks to his magical sword.

Rokujō no Miyasundokoro 六条御息所

TRANSLATION: Lady Rokujō; Miyasundokoro is her given name
ALTERNATE NAMES: Rokujō Miyasudokoro

APPEARANCE: Lady Rokujō is a woman who appears in the noh play *Aoi no Ue*, which is based on the 11th century novel *The Tale of Genji*. The novel revolves around the life of Hikaru Genji, a noble living in the height of the Heian period. Lady Rokujō's transformation from noblewoman to demoness has made her one of the most well-known monsters in Japanese theater. Her name comes from Rokujō, the area of Kyōto in which she lived.

LEGENDS: Lady Rokujō was the daughter of a minister living in the capital during the Heian period. She was high ranking, extremely beautiful, elegant, sophisticated, and intelligent. She had been married to the crown prince and would have become empress upon his ascension. However, when her husband passed away Lady Rokujō lost much of her power and standing among the court, robbing her of her ambitions. She sent their daughter away to Ise to become a shrine princess, and became a courtesan of the imperial court.

The widowed Lady Rokujō soon became one of the mistresses of an aspiring nobleman named Hikaru Genji. She fell deeply in love with him. But because of her age, rank, beauty, and refinement, Genji was reluctant to return her affections. Lady Rokujō also could not express her true feelings as she wished without breaking court decorum. Instead, she repressed her feelings of jealousy, which began to transform her into a demon.

One night, while sightseeing during the Hollyhock Festival, Lady Rokujō's carriage collided with the carriage belonging to Genji's rightful wife Lady Aoi. After already losing her place to Genji's wife, Lady Rokujō discovered that Lady Aoi was pregnant with Genji's child. The insult was too much. Her repressed jealousy escaped from her body and transformed into an ikiryō, which haunted Lady Aoi every night. Eventually, the ikiryō was witnessed by Genji, who purchased herbal charms for his wife to protect her against evil spirits.

Lady Aoi gave birth to Genji's son, but shortly afterwards became possessed by Lady Rokujō's vengeful spirit. (This possession is the subject of the noh play *Aoi no Ue*.) The ikiryō was finally exorcised by a shugenja, but the possession took its toll on Lady Aoi. She passed away.

Lady Rokujō had hoped to become Genji's next wife, but she discovered that her own hair and clothes carried the odor of Genji's herbal charms. She realized that she had been responsible for the hauntings. Thinking that Genji could never love her after murdering his wife, Lady Rokujō left the capital and joined her daughter at the Ise Shrine.

Six years later, Lady Rokujō returned to Kyōto with her daughter and became a nun. Shortly afterwards, she fell very ill. Genji came to visit her, and was stricken with her daughter. Lady Rokujō, still deeply in love with Genji, begged him not to take her daughter as a lover. Lady Rokujō passed away, and Genji adopted her daughter as his ward. They moved into her old villa at Rokujō.

Even in death, Lady Rokujō's jealousy remained as a vengeful shiryō, which appeared at the Rokujō villa. It haunted Genji, attacking his new wife Lady Murasaki and the other ladies of the house. Upon hearing of the hauntings, Lady Rokujō's daughter became sad that her mother had still not found peace in death. She performed the necessary memorial services to finally put her ghost at ease.

OBOROGURUMA 朧車

TRANSLATION: hazy cart
HABITAT: city streets, late at night
DIET: the lingering anger of ancient nobles

APPEARANCE: On misty, moonlit nights, residents of Kyōto occasionally hear the squeak of an oxcart in the street. Stepping outside to check and see, they discover a half-transparent, ghost-like oxcart with an enormous, grotesque face parked outside of their home.

ORIGIN: Carriage yōkai have existed in picture scrolls for hundreds of years. They may originally have been a kind of tsukumogami, or object-turned-yōkai. Most of these scrolls were created for their vivid imagery rather than for any particular story. Oboroguruma may have initially been created without any backstory. When Toriyama Sekien published his yōkai bestiaries, he included the oboroguruma and gave a description. He linked it to a famous scene in *The Tale of Genji* when Lady Rokujō and her rival Lady Aoi competed for a parking space and got into a carriage fight.

Long ago, sightseeing in the capital was accomplished by means of oxcart taxis. When it got crowded—particularly during festival seasons—the taxi drivers got into carriage fights. They slammed their carriages against each other to grab the best spots for sightseeing. Just like parking can be a problem in cities today, parking in ancient Kyōto was a huge source of frustration.

The resentment of nobles who didn't get the prime sightseeing spot they wanted was something to be feared. The negative feelings could build up and become a powerful force of their own, which is where these yōkai come from. Oboroguruma materialized out of the wrath of nobles who lost these carriage fights and were not able to reserve the sightseeing spots that they wanted.

KIYO HIME 清姫

TRANSLATION: Princess Kiyo

APPEARANCE: Kiyo hime is one of the most famous antagonists in Japanese literature, and an example of a honnari hannya—a demon woman who has attained the maximum level of power. She appears in *The Legend of Anchin and Kiyo Hime*, an ancient tale from Kii Province. Versions of the story appear in a number of ancient books. Her tale is retold in the famous noh play *Dōjō-ji*.

LEGENDS: Long ago, during the reign of Emperor Daigo, the young priest named Anchin was traveling from Mutsu to Kumano on a pilgrimage. Every year he made the journey, and every year he would lodge at the manor of the Masago no Shōji family. He was an incredibly good looking young man, and he caught the eye of Kiyo hime, the manor lord's daughter. She was a troublesome young girl. Anchin joked to her that if she were a good girl and behaved herself, he would marry her and take her back to Mutsu.

Every year Kiyo hime waited for Anchin to come again for his pilgrimage. When she came of age, she reminded him of his promise and asked him to marry her. Anchin, embarrassed that she had taken his word seriously, lied that he would come for her as soon as he finished his pilgrimage. On his return, he avoided the Masago no Shōji manor and headed straight for Mutsu.

When Kiyo hime heard of Anchin's deception, she was overcome with grief. She ran after the young priest, barefoot, determined to marry him. Anchin fled as fast as he could, but Kiyo hime caught him on the road to the temple Dōjō-ji. There, instead of greeting her, Anchin lied again. He pretended not to know her and protested that he was late for a meeting somewhere else. Kiyo hime's sadness turned into furious rage. She attacked, moving to punish the lying priest. Anchin prayed to Kumano Gongen to save him. A divine light dazzled Kiyo hime's eyes and paralyzed her body, giving Anchin just enough time to escape.

When Anchin reached the Hidaka River, he paid the boatman and begged him not to allow his pursuer to cross. Then, he ran to Dojō-ji for safety. Kiyo hime's rage exploded to its limits—the divine intervention had pushed her over the edge. She transformed into a giant, fire-breathing serpent. Ignoring the boatman entirely, Kiyo hime swam across the river after Anchin.

Seeing the monstrous serpent, the priests of Dōjō-ji hid Anchin inside of the large, bronze temple bell. However, Kiyo hime could smell Anchin inside. Overcome with rage and despair, she wrapped herself around the bell and breathed fire until the bronze became white hot. She roasted Anchin alive inside the bell. With Anchin dead, the demon Kiyo hime threw herself into the river and drowned.

AMIKIRI 網切

TRANSLATION: net cutter
HABITAT: villages and towns, particularly fishing villages
DIET: unknown

APPEARANCE: Amikiri are small, crustacean-like yōkai that resemble shrimp or lobsters. They have long bodies, red segmented shells, bird-like beaks, and two scissor-like claws on their forearms. They fly through the air as a fish swims in water. Amikiri are quite shy, rarely appearing before humans.

BEHAVIOR: Amikiri don't interact with humans very much, except for one particular activity—for some strange reason, amikiri love to cut nets. Whether it is a fishing net, a screen door or window, or a kaya—a hanging mosquito net—the amikiri want to cut it. That is the reason why they are called "net cutters." While they are not directly harmful, this mischief is not entirely benign. A fisherman whose nets have been shredded by an amikiri could find his livelihood ruined.

ORIGIN: It's unclear where amikiri come from. They bear a strong resemblance both in name and shape to an arthropod-like yōkai called kamikiri, which cuts women's hair. Stories about amikiri are rare, and their name and shape may actually be a pun. The word ami means net in Japanese, but it also is the name of a type of tiny shrimp.

LEGENDS: A story from Dewa Province tells of a fisherman who one day found that his fishing net had been shredded to the point of worthlessness. He suspected the work of an amikiri. The next day, he took special care to hide his nets at his home where they could not be found by any wandering yōkai. That night, however, the amikiri snuck into his room while he slept and cut up the kaya covering his bed. The man woke up with his entire body covered in painful, itchy mosquito bites.

Yama oroshi 山颪

Translation: mountain wind; sounds like mountain grater
Habitat: kitchens and gardens

Appearance: The yama oroshi is a metal grater which has been improperly cared for and has grown too dull to grate anything. It sprouts a body, and the dull slicers on the grater stick out like wild spines from its head.

Origin: Yama oroshi's name contains a double pun. First, the Japanese word for grater is *oroshi*, which is found in this tsukumogami's name. Second, its name sounds like *yamaarashi*, the Japanese word for porcupine. This yōkai resembles a porcupine with its spines.

HAHAKIGAMI 箒神

TRANSLATION: broom spirit
ALTERNATE NAMES: hōkigami
HABITAT: streets, yards, and dirty places

APPEARANCE: Hahakigami are tsukumogami which take up residence in brooms. They can sometimes be seen on cold, windy late autumn mornings, sweeping wildly at the blowing leaves.

ORIGIN: Long ago, brooms were not only household cleaning tools, but also holy instruments used in ritual purification ceremonies. They were used to sweep the air in a room in order to purify it and sweep out any evil spirits or negative energy that might be lingering. Like any tool used for many years, brooms which reach old age becomes a perfect home for spirits—perhaps even more so in the case of a hahakigami because of the ritual nature of their origin.

Hahakigami are used also as magical charms for safe and quick childbirth. Because brooms are used to "sweep out" evil energy, hahakigami act as a sort of totem to "sweep out" the baby from its mother safely. They are also used as charms to keep guests from overstaying their visit. Anyone who has stayed beyond their welcome might also be "swept out" by the power of the hahakigami.

197

Shōgorō 鉦五郎

TRANSLATION: "Gong-goro," or ghost gong, depending on the reading
HABITAT: old, dilapidated temples

APPEARANCE: Shōgorō are a kind of tsukumogami, spirits which inhabit household items. In this case, they are an animated *shōgo* (鉦吾)—small, bowl-shaped gongs that are struck with mallets and used in Buddhist services. Shōgo see a lot of use. They are struck multiple times every service. They are made of metal, and can last years without breaking. Worn out gongs sometimes cease to play their notes pleasantly. These get put into storage until forgotten. Or gongs might be the witness to some horrible crime. Either way, they are ideal candidates for awakening into yōkai.

BEHAVIOR: Like most tsukumogami, shōgorō are not dangerous. At their worst, they are startling. They wander around at night like some kind of metal turtle, striking their bodies and ringing their notes out into the night. It is enough of a racket to cause a sleepless night, but not much else.

ORIGIN: The name shōgorō is a pun. It is a combination of shōgo, the gong, and Gorō, a common boy's name. The word can also be read as a combination of shōgo and goryō, the ghost of a noble or an aristocrat from ages past. Goryō are a grade of ghost above yūrei, and play a large part in many Japanese ghost stories.

LEGENDS: In the early 18th century, there was a wealthy merchant family called Yodoya living in Osaka. For many generations, the Yodoya were the kings of the rice trade, raking in unbelievable amounts of cash. The 5th generation boss, Yodoya Tatsugorō, had so much money and lived a life of such extreme opulence that he attracted the attention of the *bakufu*, the regional shogunate officials that acted like military police.

The bakufu decided that the Yodoya family had accumulated too much wealth. They were only a merchant family, and it was improper for a lower class to have such a vast fortune; their economic power was above their station in life. The bakufu stripped Yodoya Tatsugorō of everything he had—his rice, his business, his house, his every last possession. The Yodoya family fell into ruin, and Tatsugorō became destitute. Even his favorite possession, an unbelievably rich and indescribably splendid golden chicken called *kogane no niwatori* (金の鶏, literally "golden chicken"), was taken from him. The loss of his precious golden chicken caused Tatsugorō so much grief that he died. Because of the unhappy circumstances of his death, his ghost was unable to pass on.

Normally, when a ghost lingers like this, it attaches itself to the object of its desire, be it a person, a place, or (in this case) a thing. Tatsugorō's soul meant to attach itself to his precious kogane no niwatori. In Japanese, the words for "gong" and "gold" can both be read *kane*. Poor Tatsugorō's ghost must have gotten confused and attached itself to a nearby shōgo instead of his chicken. The instrument turned into a tsukumogami.

NYOIJIZAI 如意自在

TRANSLATION: a pun meaning both "free staff" and "exactly as you please"
HABITAT: living rooms and bedrooms

APPEARANCE: Nyoijizai are *nyoi*—a kind of priest's staff—that turn into yōkai after existing for many years. They also bear a strong resemblance to *magonote*, which literally means "grandchild's hand," and refers to backscratchers. A nyoijizai's only power is its ability to scratch that itchy spot on your back which you just can't seem to reach, no matter how hard you try.

ORIGIN: Nyoijizai's name is a play on words. While nyoi is a term for a priest's staff, it can also mean "as you wish." *Jizai* means "freely" or "at will." While this name evokes an animated staff, it also literally means "exactly as you please." Thus, nyoijizai is an animated back-scratching staff that allows you to freely scratch any place you wish, exactly as you please.

ERITATEGOROMO 襟立衣

TRANSLATION: standing-collar clothes
HABITAT: temples

APPEARANCE: Eritategoromo are Buddhist high priest's kimonos that have transformed into yōkai. They still look mostly like the high-collared ceremonial robes of a priest. However the long, pointed collars have twisted into long, pointed noses, and they have sprouted eyes and beards.

ORIGIN: The most famous eritategoromo was once the kimono worn by Sōjōbō, King of the Tengu, who lives on Mount Kurama, north of Kyōto. Sōjōbō is a fearsome, powerful, wise, god-like monster, with the strength of 1000 ordinary tengu. He is a master swordsman, and was responsible for training a number of famous legendary heroes of Japan, such as Minamoto no Yoshitsune. Though he is an ascetic yamabushi and great teacher, like any tengu, Sōjōbō has an evil side too. He is said to feed on children who wander too deep into the mountains.

Sōjōbō was not always a tengu. He was born a human, and became a well-respected high priest. He was also proud. He mistakenly believed that he had achieved satori, or enlightenment. Though he expected to become a Buddha when he died, he transformed instead into a demonic tengu. Even as a tengu, the proud Sōjōbō continued to live as a Buddhist priest. He trained daily, and wearing his ornate priestly vestments. Either due to Sōjōbō's extreme pride, or due to being worn by a magical tengu, a spirit became attached to his high-collared robes. They transformed into this yōkai.

YANARI 家鳴

TRANSLATION: house squeaker
HABITAT: wooden houses, especially new construction
DIET: unknown

APPEARANCE: Yanari are miniature oni which appear in houses late at night. They live most often in wooden houses—especially those of cheap or new construction in which all of the parts have not had time to settle yet. Yanari often carry miniature weapons or tools, such as mallets or iron clubs.

BEHAVIOR: Yanari only do one thing, and they love doing it—making noise. They come out from the floors, ceilings, and the woodwork late at night when everyone is in bed. They run about the house performing mischief. Specifically, yanari bang the furniture, walls, floors, ceilings, and anything else they can find. Although they are usually non-destructive, occasionally they break things. Yanari delight in the work, and take it very seriously. Although tiny, they have a strong work ethic and do their best to perform their duty of making noise to the fullest.

LEGENDS: Long ago, in Tajima Province, a group of ronin decided to test their courage by spending a night in a haunted house. Late at night, when they were fast asleep, the entire house suddenly began to shake violently. The ronin, thinking it was an earthquake, dashed outside for safety. However, they soon realized that theirs was the only house shaking.

The next day the ronin visited a wise man who lived nearby and told him of their experience at the haunted house. The wise man offered to stay with them that night to see for himself. Sure enough, late at night, the entire house shook violently. The wise man looked carefully at the floor. Locating the area where the most violent shaking was originating, he stabbed his dagger deep into the tatami mat. Suddenly, the house was quiet.

The next morning, the ronin and the wise man examined the house. Under the floor where the wise man had stabbed his dagger they found a strange gravestone dedicated to the memory of a bear. Where the knife had penetrated the stone tablet, blood was trickling out.

The wise man asked others in the neighborhood what the strange gravestone could mean. They explained that some time ago there was a bear in these parts who broke into peoples' houses at night. One night it broke into that particular house, and the man who lived in there killed it. In order to appease the spirit of the bear and protect himself from its vengeful ghost, the man had a gravestone placed in the house dedicated to the bear's memory. The ghost of the bear must have possessed that gravestone, which caused the yanari to appear every night and shake the house.

SAKABASHIRA 逆柱

TRANSLATION: upside-down pillar
HABITAT: houses
DIET: none; it lives off of its own resentment

APPEARANCE: Sakabashira are the angry spirits of tree leaves which manifest inside houses where one of the pillars has been placed upside-down—that is to say, in the opposite direction of the way the tree was pointing when it was living. These spirits manifest their grudge late at night, and bring misfortune upon those living in the house.

BEHAVIOR: Sakabashira are most well-known for making noises. They creak and moan, imitate the sounds of wooden beams cracking, and sometimes even speak in sentences like, "My neck hurts!" They can cause houses to shake, and the leaf-spirits residing in the tree can manifest as yanari. They act like poltergeists and break things around the house. Sakabashira can be so loud that families move out of a house. These yōkai cause not only strange noises, but also terrible luck. People who stay in a house haunted by sakabashira often lose their family fortunes, or even see all of their possessions consumed in great conflagrations which destroy the cursed house.

ORIGIN: It has long been a folk belief that a pillar erected in the upside-down position will bring misfortune. Sakabashira are usually the result of a careless mistake on the part of the construction crew. In order to prevent this yōkai from appearing, folk superstition tells us that a pillar must be erected in the same orientation as the tree had when it was alive. However, sometimes support pillars are actually installed upside-down way on purpose. This is due to another folk belief: "The moment a house is completed, it starts to fall apart." As a kind of ward against bad luck, Japanese buildings were sometimes only almost completed, with the final step being left out, or purposefully made into a mistake. The famous shrine Nikko Tōshō-gū is one example. It was built with just one pillar purposefully pointing in the opposite direction. This same superstition was followed when building the imperial palace—placing the final pillar in an upside-down position. During the Edo period, house builders commonly "forgot" to place the last three roof tiles for the same reason.

Tenjō kudari 天井下

TRANSLATION: ceiling hanger
ALTERNATE NAMES: tenjō sagari, tenzurushi
HABITAT: attics and roof crawlspaces
DIET: unknown; possibly humans

APPEARANCE: Tenjō kudari has the appearance of a naked, ugly, old woman with a long tongue, and long, disheveled hair. This yōkai was first documented by Toriyama Sekien. Aside from his illustration, little else is known about it.

BEHAVIOR: Tenjō kudari spends most of its time in hiding. It lives in the narrow crawl space between the ceiling and the roof. Every so often, in the middle of the night, it crawls out from the ceiling, upside-down, to scare people.

ORIGIN: In old Japan, the space above the ceiling was connected with superstitions and legends about dead bodies rolling about at night or women being confined like prisoners. Tenjō kudari seems to have been something Toriyama invented based on those myths. During his time, the phrase "to show someone the ceiling" was a colloquial expression for causing trouble—which tenjō kudari certainly does.

A few possible connections to origins outside of Toriyama's imagination exist. One involves the story of a yōkai that moved into the roof crawl space of an inn in Yamanashi. During the night, it descended from the ceiling and snatched up travelers to eat. However, it isn't certain whether this myth inspired Toriyama Sekien, or rather was inspired by his work.

MAKURAGAESHI 枕返し

TRANSLATION: pillow flipper
ALTERNATE NAMES: makura kozō
HABITAT: bedrooms
DIET: none; as a ghost it does not eat

APPEARANCE: Makuragaeshi are a kind of zashiki warashi—child ghosts which haunt specific rooms of a house. Though details vary from region to region, they are found all over Japan. They take the form of a small child dressed as a *Niō* (Buddhist guardian deities), a monk, or a samurai, and appear in bedrooms late at night.

BEHAVIOR: Makuragaeshi are named for their primary activity—flipping pillows. People who sleep in a room haunted by makuragaeshi often wake up to find that their pillow has been flipped and is now at their feet. Makuragaeshi are also known for other minor pranks, such as running through ashes and leaving dirty footprints around the rooms they haunt.

While most stories about makuragaeshi present them as harmless pranksters, there are a few stories that describe scarier powers. Some don't flip the pillow, but lift up and flip people instead. Others pick up entire tatami mats that people are sleeping on and bounce them around. Still others are said to sit on their victim's chest while he or she sleeps, pressing down hard and squeezing the wind out of the lung. They occasionally cause kanashibari, or sleep paralysis. The most extreme stories say that anyone who sees a makuragaeshi loses consciousness. After they pass out the makuragaeshi steals their souls, leaving them dead.

ORIGIN: There are as many theories as to where makuragaeshi come from as there are variants of zashiki warashi. Most often they linked to the ghosts of people—particularly children—who died in the room they come to haunt. As makuragaeshi are lower in rank than zashiki warashi, they are often the result of ghosts which died tragically, such as murder victims. However, some makuragaeshi have also been attributed to shape-shifting, prank-loving yōkai such as tanuki or *saru* (monkeys). Others still have attributed this spirit to the actions of monster cats such as kasha.

ABURA AKAGO 油赤子

TRANSLATION: oil baby
HABITAT: human-inhabited areas
DIET: lamp oil

APPEARANCE: Abura akago are yōkai from Ōmi Province. They are a type of hi no tama, or fireball, but can also take on the shape of a baby.

BEHAVIOR: Abura akago first appear as mysterious orbs of fire which float aimlessly through the night sky. They drift from house to house and—upon entering one—transform into small babies. In this baby form, they lick the oil from oil lamps and paper lanterns, known as andon. They then turn back into orbs and fly away.

ORIGIN: Like many other oil-related yōkai, abura akago are said to originate from oil thieves. While the particular circumstances of these oil thieves are lost to time, they mirror so many other yōkai that we can infer that these thieves died and—instead of passing on to the next life—turned into yōkai as a penalty for their sins.

HIKESHI BABA 火消婆

TRANSLATION: fire extinguishing old woman
HABITAT: human-inhabited areas
DIET: unknown; probably omnivorous

APPEARANCE: Hikeshi baba takes the form of a white-haired, grotesque-looking, old woman. She wanders from house to house blowing out lanterns.

INTERACTIONS: Hikeshi baba is not a dangerous yōkai herself, although her actions can indirectly harm people. Her purpose is to make the world a gloomier place by extinguishing the cheerful, beautiful paper lanterns that decorate Japanese homes. Yōkai, by nature, are not accustomed to bright lights or cheery atmospheres. Her work is intended to make conditions more suitable for other yōkai to come out and do their own misdeeds.

KANBARI NYŪDŌ 加牟波理入道

TRANSLATION: kanbari priest; the meaning is unknown
ALTERNATE NAMES: ganbari nyūdō
HABITAT: bathrooms
DIET: omnivorous

APPEARANCE: Kanbari nyūdō is a perverted ghost-like yōkai which lurks outside of bathrooms on New Year's Eve. It has a roughly priest-like appearance, with robes and a tonsured haircut. Its body is covered in thick hairs. Kanbari nyūdō blows a cuckoo out of its mouth. As it only comes out once per year, very little is known about this yōkai.

INTERACTIONS: There are many conflicting accounts about what kanbari nyūdō actually does. What is certain is that it lurks outside of bathrooms on New Year's Eve, and peeks into the window at people using the toilet. What happens next varies from place to place. In general, this yōkai brings bad luck in the coming year. In more recent stories, kanbari nyūdō tries to stroke or lick the person using the toilet. Sometimes, it inflicts constipation upon those who see it.

ORIGIN: Kanbari nyūdō's history and origins are confused and convoluted. According to Toriyama Sekien, this yōkai originally comes from the Chinese god of the toilet, Kakutō. Because the characters used to write Kakutō are similar to the characters used to write the Japanese word for cuckoo, this may have been intended as a pun on Sekien's part. However, Kakutō was not, in fact, a Chinese toilet god. He was actually a 15th century Ming general.

The cuckoo connection does actually trace back to China. It was considered bad luck to hear a cuckoo's call in the toilet—if you hear a cuckoo while using the toilet, you have to bark like a dog to counter the curse.

This yōkai's name is also a mystery. It can be written in many different ways using many different kanji, although none of them have a particular meaning. They appear to be ateji—kanji chosen solely for their phonetic readings. Jippensha Ikku, an Edo period author, wrote about ganbari nyūdō using kanji meaning "stretched eyes"—very appropriate considering this yōkai's propensity for peeping. However, as no earlier stories use those kanji for the name, it is certainly his own (very clever) fabrication. Ganbari may also be connected to the word *ganbaru*, which means to try hard and persevere—which may or may not be related to certain bathroom activities. But this is almost certainly a connection made after the fact, rather than being the origin of this yōkai's name.

LEGENDS: Stories about kanbari nyūdō differ wildly from region to region. According to some local legends, if you enter an outhouse on New Year's Eve at the hour of the ox, between 1 and 3 am, and peer down into the hole and chant "*ganbari nyūdō*" three times, a human head will appear in the hole. If you then take that head and insert it into your left kimono sleeve and then take it back out, it will turn into a *koban*—an oval-shaped gold coin. In other regions, the human head must instead be wrapped up inside of a silk cloth and taken back to one's room. When the cloth is unwrapped, it will be filled with gold.

In most areas, kanbari nyūdō are thought to be bringers of bad luck. If one enters the toilet on New Year's Eve and chants the spell, "*ganbari nyūdō, hototogisu!*" ("ganbari priest, cuckoo!") this yōkai will not appear, and thus the following year will not be unlucky. On the other hand, in other areas, chanting the same phrase or even remembering those magic words is unlucky enough to guarantee an entire year of bad luck.

Kurote 黒手

TRANSLATION: black hand
HABITAT: toilets
DIET: omnivorous

APPEARANCE: A kurote is a bizarre, hairy yōkai from the Noto peninsula in Ishikawa Prefecture.

LEGENDS: Long ago in Noto Province, there was a samurai named Kasamatsu Jingobei. He lived in a nice house, as was typical of samurai at the time. One day, his wife went to use the bathroom, and something strange happened. While using the toilet, she felt a hand reach up from the darkness and stroke her behind. She told her husband, who suspected the work of a mischievous tanuki or kitsune. Jingobei drew his katana and entered the bathroom. Sure enough, as he stood over the toilet, something moved—an arm, covered in thick, black hair, reached up out of the darkness and began making a stroking motion. With one swing of his sword, Jingobei sliced the hand clean off. He put it into a box.

Several days later, three yōkai disguised as priests appeared at Jingobei's house. Not realizing their true form, Jingobei invited them in. The first priest said, "There is a strange presence in this house..."

Jingobei brought out the box and showed them the hand. The second priest said, "This is the hand of a creature known as a kurote who lives in humans' toilets."

The third priest examined the hand closely and snarled, "This is my hand which you cut from my arm!" He immediately transformed into a 9-foot tall, black-haired monster. He snatched the hand away, and then all three priests vanished.

Sometime later, while Jingobei was walking home late at night, something like a quilt fell down from the sky on top of him. Wrapped up and unable to move, Jingobei was lifted up seven feet into the air and then violently slammed to the ground. When he came to, Jingobei noticed that the sword he was carrying on his belt—the one which he used to cut off the kurote's hand—was missing.

Ikiryō 生霊

TRANSLATION: living ghost
ALTERNATE NAMES: shōryō, seirei, ikisudama
DIET: none; lives off its creator's emotions

APPEARANCE: Ikiryō are the souls of still-living people that have temporarily left their bodies and move about on their own. They appear just as the living person from which they spawn. Sometimes they take on a ghostly, translucent form. Other times they are indistinguishable from a living person.

INTERACTIONS: There are a number of ways for ikiryō to appear—during a near-death-experience, fainting, intense passion or desire, intense hatred, or even as part of a curse. Ikiryō most commonly appear due to some intense emotion or trauma. The owner of the soul is almost always unaware of the ikiryō's existence. This can lead to some awkward situations and misunderstandings.

Folk superstitions about ikiryō go back to before recorded history. According to ancient superstition, just before death the soul leaves the body and is able to walk around, making strange noises and doing other things outside of the body. This is especially common during wartime. The ikiryō of soldiers in far off lands are said to appear to their friends and loved ones moments before or after their deaths, in their war uniforms, to give one last goodbye. The souls of the soon-to-die and recently-deceased are also sometimes seen visiting nearby temples and praying for a few days after their deaths.

During the Heian period, ikiryō were a popular subject of stories. They were attributed to intense feelings of love. When a person—usually a woman—felt intense passion and love, her spirit detached from her body and haunted the object of her affection. She might whisper sweet things into his ears. Depending on the strength of her feelings, the ikiryō could even physically move her lover around. This was not romantic, however—people haunted in this way were often tormented to the point of extreme sickness by these ghosts.

The most common type ikiryō is born out of rage and jealousy. Just as the ghosts of the dead can go after those who wrong them in life, an ikiryō can manifest from one living person to curse another. These are also usually unconscious manifestations. However, a few famous examples of conscious manifestations of ikiryō curses exist. The shrine visit at the hour of the ox (ushi no koku mairi) and ichijama (from Okinawa) are ceremonial curses in which a person consciously sends their soul from their body to hurt or to kill their enemies. Of course, this sort of black magic often has dire consequences for the performer as well as the target.

During the Edo period, ikiryō were considered a symptom of certain illnesses, such as the aptly-named *rikonbyō*, or "detached soul syndrome," and *kage no yamai*, or "shadow illness." These horrifyingly-named diseases were Edo period terms for sleepwalking and out-of-body experiences. For carriers of these illnesses, it was said that the soul could depart from the body at night, taking the person's consciousness along with it. This would cause them to experience things from the ikiryō's perspective as if they were actually doing it. A person might have false memories of things he didn't do, or be accused of things he didn't remember. Some people even experienced meeting their own selves, as if they had a doppelganger.

Superstitions about ikiryō have persisted into modern times, particularly those dealing with people appearing to family members and friends on or around the times of their deaths. The idea of the soul leaving the body and experiencing things during out of body experiences persists as well, and remains an unexplained phenomenon.

SHIRYŌ 死霊

TRANSLATION: dead ghost
ALTERNATE NAMES: shirei
DIET: none; thrives solely on its emotions

APPEARANCE: Shiryō are the ghosts of the dead. They contrast with ikiryō, the ghosts of the living. Shiryō is generally synonymous with yūrei ("faint spirit"), as they both refer to the classic Japanese ghost. However while yūrei can be creepy sometimes and beautifully mysterious at other times, shiryō is almost exclusively used to refer to unpleasant, malevolent spirits. The inclusion of the kanji for "death" in the name is the clue that this ghost is not to be romanticized.

INTERACTIONS: Shiryō act in similar ways to ikiryō, appearing to relatives or close friends of the deceased. While ikiryō usually appear in the moments just before death, a shiryō appears in the moments just after death. When one appears, it is most often to give one last goodbye to its loved ones before departing. However, shiryō do not always appear in order to say goodbye; sometimes they come to take their loved ones away with them into the world of the dead.

LEGENDS: Belief in shiryō goes back to before recorded history. They have long been a staple of Japanese folk superstition. One famous account is recorded in *Tōno Monogatari*, a 1910 collection of folk beliefs which gave birth to the field of academic folklore research in Japan. In this story, there was a young girl who lived together with her father. After her father died, his shiryō appeared before the young girl and tried to take her with him into the world of the dead. The girl narrowly escaped and fled from the house to ask for help. Every night, various friends and distant family members agreed to stay overnight in the house with her and watch over her. Every night without fail, her father's shiryō came looking for her, to try to take her away. Only after a whole month of sleepless, terrifying nights did the ghost stop appearing. Finally the girl was left in peace.

225

Goryō 御霊

TRANSLATION: honored ghost
ALTERNATE NAMES: mitama
DIET: none; exists solely for vengeance

APPEARANCE: Goryō are the ghosts of ancient warriors and nobles who died horrible, agonizing deaths and returned to haunt their enemies as dreadful ghosts of vengeance called onryō.

INTERACTIONS: These terrible ghosts bring calamity and destruction to those who wronged them in life. Their revenge is often in the form of fires, wars, plagues, droughts, floods, storms, the deaths of imperial family members, and other disasters which the ancient nobility viewed as curses. Because ghosts cannot be killed, the only way to end their wrath was to transform them into peaceful, benevolent spirits. This was done with the help of priests and onmyōji, through the religion known as goryō shinkō—the religion of ghosts.

THE RELIGION OF GHOSTS

Onryō were one of the most terrifying things to Heian period nobles. This explains the great lengths gone to pacify them—often by the very people who caused their deaths. The Heian period was a volatile time, with frequent revolts, succession crises, political scheming, and wars. Many noble families saw their fortunes rise and fall at the expense of others. The belief that one's enemies could harm them even after death weighed heavy.

Goryō shinkō refers to superstitious traditions which had been developing in Japan since prehistoric times. These traditions developed into a highly ritualized and important religion during the Heian period. It is the art of pacifying, and often deifying, the souls of the angered dead. Goryō—also called mitama—literally means "honored spirits." In regards to Goryō shinkō, it refers to the ghosts of aristocrats who were dishonored politically, killed in battle, or otherwise died in anguish. These unfortunates turned into vengeful onryō, came back for revenge against those who wronged them, and were pacified, enshrined, and transformed into deities.

After the Heian period, goryō shinkō began to decline. As the power of the samurai caste grew, Buddhism gradually supplanted the older rituals and superstitions that were popular with the imperial nobility. But belief in the power of onryō remained. Ghost stories about vengeful onryō remained popular throughout Japan's history, and experienced a major revival during the Edo period.

TATARIGAMI 祟り神

TRANSLATION: curse god, curse spirit
DIET: vengeance

APPEARANCE: Tatarigami are powerful spirits which bring death and destruction, fire and famine, plague, war, and all forms of calamity. They are some of the most powerful evil spirits that haunt Japan, and have done much to shape the culture and politics over the country's long history. Tatarigami can refer to powerful gods of destruction, or to the ghosts of powerful people. Famous tatarigami include gods such as Emperor Gozu, the bull-headed demon god, and Yamata no Orochi, the eight-headed eight-tailed dragon. Also included are the onryō of important historical figures such as Mononobe no Moriya, Emperor Sutoku, Sugawara no Michizane, and Taira no Masakado. In the case of historical figures, they are almost always ancient nobles who died in anguish and transformed into onryō.

INTERACTIONS: Tatarigami wreak havoc upon those who wronged them—usually other nobles. In order to appease their vengeful spirits, shrines honoring them have been built across Japan. Through proper appeasement, their curses can be lifted, or at least abated.

The Gion Matsuri in Kyōto, one of the most famous festivals in Japan, is an example of a ceremony initially designed to appease a tatarigami. During the Heian period, Kyōto suffered a number of outbreaks which were thought to be caused by Susanoo and Gozu tennō—two powerful gods of disease and destruction. In order to appease their wrath, a festival was held in their honor at the Yasaka Shrine in Gion. To keep the city free from disease, the festival was repeated every year. Eventually the connection to Susanoo and Emperor Gozu was lost, but the festival traditions remain to this day.

The appeasement of tatarigami remained an important part of religious life throughout the Heian period and beyond. The duty of pacifying these curse spirits fell to the onmyōji, and popular belief in this superstition helped onmyōdō rise in power.

SANSHI 三尸

TRANSLATION: the three corpses; the three spirits

APPEARANCE: The sanshi are three spiritual worms found inside of humans. Each is about 6 centimeters long. These worms live in their hosts from the moment they are born to the moment they die. They work hard to cause their hosts to do evil things.

INTERACTIONS: The names of the sanshi are Jōshi, Chūshi, and Geshi, meaning upper worm, middle worm, and lower worm. Jōshi lives in your head and looks like a Taoist wise man. He is responsible for making your eyes grow weak, creating wrinkles, and growing white hairs. Chūshi lives in your torso and looks like a wild beast. He is responsible for damaging internal organs, making you overeat and overdrink, and causing bad dreams. Geshi lives in the lower half of your body and looks like a human foot with a cow's head. He drains the will and shortens the life of his host.

The number 60 is an important number in Chinese astrology, and every sixty days the sanshi leave the body to visit the King of Heaven while their host human sleeps. They report their host's wicked deeds for the year to king. Depending on this report, the King of Heaven shortens each human's life span by a certain amount.

To escape the King of Heaven's sentence, Kōshin practitioners do not sleep every 60th night, so the sanshi are never able to leave the body and give their report. Additionally, spells and charms are chanted to prevent any harm done by the sanshi. The following spell is said to defeat the sanshi:

ホウコウシ、ホウジョウシ メイコシ シツニュウヨウメイイチュウ キョリガシン
HO-U-KO-U-SHI, HO-U-JO-U-SHI ME-I-KO-SHI
SHI-TSU-NYU-U-YO-U-ME-I-I-CHU-U KYO-RI-GA-SHI-N

Finally, if you find yourself drowsy and unable to stay awake, the following spell must be chanted:

シヤムシハ、イネヤサリネヤ ワガトコヲ ネタレヅネヌゾ ネネドネタレルゾ
SHI-YA-MU-SHI-HA, I-NE-YA-SA-RI-NE-YA WA-GA-TO-KO-WO
NE-TA-RE-ZO-NE-NU-ZO NE-NE-DO-NE-TA-RE-RU-ZO

KŌSHIN

The sanshi derive from Taoist beliefs, many of which were incorporated into Japanese folk religions. The most well-known of these is Kōshin, a religion with Taoist, Shinto, and Buddhist origins mixed with local folk traditions. The custom of staying up all night during Kōshin nights is called Kōshin machi and became popular among the aristocracy of the Heian period. They stayed up together in large groups to help pass the time and prevent sleepiness. Kōshin machi soon evolved into an all-night eating and drinking party. Belief in Kōshin enjoyed a resurgence in popularity during the Edo period, as members of all classes began to practice certain aspects of the religion.

Today, Kōshin is less well-known. Most Kōshin temples have been absorbed into Buddhist temple complexes. However, many elements still remain hidden in plain sight. Perhaps the most well-known symbol of Kōshin is the statue of the three wise monkeys Mizaru, Kikazaru, and Iwazaru—the see-no-evil, hear-no-evil, say-no-evil monkeys.

ABE NO SEIMEI 安倍晴明

APPEARANCE: Abe no Seimei is perhaps the most famous onmyōji in Japanese history. A descendent of the famous poet Abe no Nakamaro, he lived from 921 to 1005 CE. Due to his success as an astrologer and diviner, he was widely believed to be a genius—and a wielder of magical powers and secret knowledge.

ORIGIN: Abe no Seimei's fame comes from the success he had as an onmyōji in the 10th century. He was a student of Kamo no Tadayuki and Kamo no Yasunori, and succeeded Yasunori as astrologer and diviner for the imperial court. Seimei's duties included foreseeing the gender of unborn babies, diving the location of objects, advising on matters of personal conduct, conducting exorcisms and crafting wards against dark magic and evil spirits, and analyzing and interpreting events such as celestial phenomena. He wrote numerous books on divination and fortune telling, including Senji Ryakketsu, containing six thousand forecast and thirty-six fortune telling techniques using shikigami, and a translation of Hoki Naiden, detailing secret divination techniques.

Abe no Seimei was so renowned that the Abe family remained in control of the Bureau of Onmyō until it was shut down in 1869. After his death, stories about Seimei began to spread rapidly and continued to do so for hundreds of years. Eventually, the details of his life became so intertwined with countless legends that the truth was no longer distinguishable from myth.

LEGENDS: It was believed that Abe no Seimei's magical aptitude derived from a supernatural lineage. His mother was said to be a kitsune, making him half-yōkai. Seimei's father, Abe no Yasuna, saved a white fox which was being chased by hunters. The fox transformed into a beautiful human woman and said her name was Kuzunoha. Out of thanks for saving her life, Kuzunoha became Yasuna's wife and bore him a son, Seimei.

By age five, Abe no Seimei's yōkai lineage was becoming apparent. He was able to command weak oni and force them to do his bidding. One day, he witnessed his mother in her fox form. Kuzunoha explained to Seimei that she was the white fox his father once saved. She then fled into the forest, never to return again. Kuzunoha entrusted her son to the onmyōji Kamo no Tadayuki in order to ensure that he would not grow up to be evil.

Abe no Seimei had many rivals. One of them was a famous priest from Harima named Chitoku Hōshi. Chitoku was a skilled sorcerer, and wanted to test Seimei to see if he was truly as great as people said he was. Chitoku disguised himself as a traveler and visited Seimei's house, and asked Seimei to teach him magic. Seimei saw through the disguise instantly. Even more, he saw that the two servants Chitoku had brought with him were shikigami—summoned servant spirits—in disguise.

Seimei decided to have a little bit of fun with Chitoku. He agreed to train him, but said that it was not a good day, and that he should come back tomorrow. Chitoku went back to his home, while unbeknownst to him, Seimei unsummoned both of the shikigami. The next day, Chitoku realized that his servants were gone, and he approached Seimei to ask him to return his shikigami. Seimei laughed at him, angrily scolding him for trying to trick him. Any other person, he said, would not be so kind to return shikigami that were employed against him! Chitoku realized that he was in way over his head; not only could Seimei see through his disguise, but he was able to manipulate all of his spells as well. He bowed low, begged for forgiveness, and offered to become Seimei's servant.

Abe no Seimei's chief rival was a sorcerer from Harima named Ashiya Dōman. Dōman was much older than Seimei, and believed that there was no one in the land who was a better onmyōji than he was. Upon hearing of Seimei's genius, he challenged him to a magical duel.

On the day of the competition, many officials and witnesses came to watch. The two sorcerers met in the imperial gardens for the contest. First, Dōman picked up a handful of sand, concentrated over it for a moment, and threw it into the air. The particles of sand turned into countless swallows which began to flit around the garden. Seimei waved his folding fan one time, and all of the swallows turned back into grits of sand.

Next, Seimei recited a spell. A dragon appeared in the sky above. Rain began to fall all around them. Dōman recited his spell, however as hard as he tried, he could not cause the dragon to vanish. Instead, the rain grew fiercer and fiercer, filling the garden with water up to Dōman's waist. Finally, Seimei cast his spell again. The rain stopped, and the dragon vanished.

The third and final contest was a divination challenge: the contestants had to guess the contents of a wooden box. Dōman, indignant at having lost the previous round, challenged Seimei: "Whoever loses this round will become the other's servant!" Dōman confidently declared that there were 15 oranges inside of the box. Seimei contradicted him, saying that there were 15 rats in the box. The emperor and his attendants who had prepared the test shook their heads, for they had put 15 oranges in the box. They announced that Seimei had lost. However, when they opened the box, 15 rats leaped out! Not only had Seimei divined the contents of the box, he had transformed the oranges into rats, tricking Dōman and the entire court. Victory went to Seimei.

Ashiya Dōman continued to hold a grudge against Abe no Seimei, and continued to plot against him. He seduced Seimei's wife and convinced her to tell him Seimei's magical secrets. She showed him the stone box in which Seimei kept Hoki Naiden, his book of spells. Hoki Naiden was a book of secrets which had been passed down since time immemorial from India to Tang, China. It came into the possession of the Japanese envoy, Kibi no Makibi. When Kibi no Makibi returned to Japan from Tang, he presented the secret book to the relatives of his friend Abe no Nakamaro, who remained in China. From there it was passed down and eventually inherited by Abe no Seimei.

One night when Seimei returned home, Dōman boasted that he had acquired Seimei's secret magic book. Seimei scolded him, saying that was impossible. So impossible, in fact, that if Dōman did have the book, he could cut Seimei's throat. Dōman triumphantly presented the book, and Seimei, realizing that he had been betrayed by his wife, offered his throat to Dōman. Dōman gladly cut it open. Seimei died.

When Seimei was murdered, Saint Hokudō—the Chinese wizard who had given Hoki Naiden to Kibi no Makibi—sensed the loss of a great sorcerer. He traveled across the sea to Japan, collected Seimei's bones, and restored Abe no Seimei to life. The pair of them set out to get revenge on Dōman and Seimei's ex-wife, who was now married to Dōman.

Saint Hokudō paid a visit to Seimei's home, where Dōman and his wife were now living. He asked if Abe no Seimei was home, to which Dōman replied that, unfortunately, Abe no Seimei had been murdered some time ago. Saint Hokudō said that was impossible, for he had just seen Seimei earlier that day. Dōman laughed at him, saying that was impossible. So impossible, in fact, that if Seimei was actually alive, he could cut Dōman's throat. Saint Hokudō called out to Abe no Seimei, who presented himself. He then promptly cut open the throats of Ashiya Dōman and his wife.

Today, Abe no Seimei is worshipped as a god at many shrines throughout Japan. His main shrine is located in Kyōto, and sits on the site of his former house.

Taira no Masakado 平将門

APPEARANCE: Taira no Masakado was a samurai of the Heian period, a powerful warrior, and a great leader. He was born either in the late 800s or early 900s CE and was killed in 940. After his death, his spirit is said to have returned as a vengeful ghost and brought destruction across the country. Along with Emperor Sutoku and Sugawara no Michizane, he is one of the *Nihon San Dai Onryō*—Three Great Onryō of Japan.

Though Taira no Masakado's birth date is unknown, he is believed to have been born sometime around when Sugawara no Michizane died. A Meiji period biography of Taira no Masakado suggests that he may have been Sugawara no Michizane's reincarnation; his revolt against the emperor may actually have been a continuation of Michizane's curse.

ORIGIN: Taira no Masakado was born into the Kanmu Heishi, the clan of Taira descended from Emperor Kanmu. It was an elite family. Masakado had a privileged childhood in the capital, after which he settled down in Shimōsa Province in Eastern Japan, northeast of modern day Tōkyō. His troubles only began after his father died. Inheritance laws at this time were not firmly established, and his uncles tried to steal most of his father's land. They claimed their royal lineage gave them the right to do so.

In 935 CE, the dispute with his family members broke into outright battle. Masakado was ambushed by one of his uncles and a number of Minamoto warriors. But Masakado was a powerful warrior. He quickly defeated them, and then took his revenge by burning their lands, ravaging the countryside, and slaughtering thousands. This brought him into conflict with other relatives by blood and by marriage, who brought their dispute to the emperor.

Taira no Masakado was summoned to court to answer charges of the relatives of the dead Minamoto warriors. Masakado was not only brave, he was also smart. He had taken great pains to remain within the law and proved that he had good reason for his killings. After only a few months, he was fully pardoned when the court offered a general amnesty in commemoration of Emperor Suzaku's coming of age.

Taira no Masakado returned to his home, but soon found himself under attack. This time, it was his father-in-law and his relatives. Again, Masakado quickly defeated them. To avoid stirring up more political trouble, Masakado received a warrant to apprehend his attackers. Now, with legal sanction for his military action, he stormed into their lands on a quest for revenge.

In 938 CE, Taira no Masakado received another court summons for questioning about a quarrel with one of the cousins who had attacked him. This time, Masakado ignored the summons. He raised a large force and invaded Hitachi Province. He conquered eight provinces: Shimotsuke, Kōzuke, Musashi, Kazusa, Awa, Sagami, Izu, and Shimōsa. The whole time, he maintained his innocence, insisting that his campaign was legal under the terms of his warrant.

The government was seen as ineffectual and the nobles as abusive by the peasants of the time. Taira no Masakado, on the other hand, treated the peasants of his conquered domains much better than their former masters did. His insurrection was seen as a salvation by many peasants. They welcomed him gladly. The court feared that Taira no Masakado was preparing to overthrow the government and declare himself the new emperor of Japan. He was condemned as a rebel and a traitor.

A number of warriors—including Masakado's ally Fujiwara no Hidesato and some his own relatives—were commissioned by the government to take his head. They caught up with

Masakado's army in Shimōsa Province on the fourteenth day of the second month of 940 CE. They attacked during a night ambush and quickly defeated the rebels. Masakado's men were outnumbered ten to one. Masakado was beheaded, betrayed by his friends and family. The head was brought back to Kyōto to be displayed in the east market as a message to would-be rebels.

LEGENDS: Strangely, Taira no Masakado's head did not decompose. Many months after it was first displayed in the east market, it still looked as fresh as the day it was severed. The eyes had grown fiercer, and the mouth twisted up into a hideous grimace. Night after night the head would call out, "Where is my murdered body!? Come here! Reattach my head and let me fight once again!" And then things got really strange.

One night the head began to glow. It flew off into the sky, across the country, towards Shimōsa. The head eventually grew tired and landed to rest in a fishing village called Shibazaki (which would one day grow into the city of Edo). The villagers who found the head cleaned it and buried it. A shrine was erected over the grave and named *Kubizuka*—the mound of the head. Masakado was honored and worshipped by the peasants as a true warrior, a symbol of justice who stood in heroic defiance of a corrupt and lazy nobility. He was seen as an underdog who was repeatedly betrayed and eventually murdered by those he should have been able to trust. Despite his deification and popularity among the lower classes, his ghost was not appeased. A few years after his head was buried, the ghost of a samurai began to be seen in the neighborhood of his shrine.

In the early 1300s, a great plague struck Edo. Many people died. The plague was attributed to Taira no Masakado's anger. In order to appease him, his spirit was moved from his small shrine to the larger and more prestigious Kanda Shrine. He was designated one of the main gods, and his spirit was placated—for a while. In 1874, Emperor Meiji visited the Kanda Shrine. It was viewed as inappropriate for an enemy of the imperial family like Masakado to be honored when the emperor was visiting, and so his deity status was revoked. His shrine was moved to a smaller building outside of the main shrine.

Taira no Masakado's anger returned in 1928. After the Great Kanto Earthquake destroyed much of the city, the site of his Kubizuka was chosen as the temporary location for the Ministry of Finance. Shortly afterwards, the Minister of Finance became sick and died. Over a dozen other employees died, and even more became sick or were injured in falls and accidents in the building. Rumors about the curse ran began to spread. The Ministry of Finance building was demolished and a memorial service for Masakado was held at the Kanda Shrine.

Throughout the 20th century, a number of other accidents, fires, sicknesses, and mysterious sightings were attributed to the curse of Taira no Masakado. Each time, purification rituals were performed. Finally, in 1984, in response to public pressure, his deity status was reinstated. Today, great pains are taken not to anger his ghost. For example, it is common practice for television stations to visit the grave of his head, still located in what is now Otemachi, Tōkyō. They pay their respects to him before his character appears on any show. The Kubizuka is maintained by an organization of local businesses and volunteers who have taken on the responsibility of upkeeping of his grave.

Many statues of frogs decorate Taira no Masakado's gravesite. The Japanese word for frog, *kaeru*, is a homophone of the word meaning "return." Just as Masakado's severed head returned to his hometown, people pray to his spirit that their loved ones will *kaeru*—return—safely. It is also said that the frogs may symbolize the frog magic that the wizard Nikushisen taught to Masakado's daughter, Takiyasha hime.

TAKIYASHA HIME 滝夜叉姫

TRANSLATION: Princess Takiyasha; literally "waterfall demon princess"

APPEARANCE: Takiyasha hime is the daughter of Taira no Masakado and a sorceress who raised an army of yōkai and attempted to conquer Japan. Her story became popular in the Edo period, and is depicted in novels, woodblock prints, and kabuki. The details of her story vary quite a bit from version to version.

LEGENDS: After Taira no Masakado was defeated and his rebellion quashed, the imperial court declared Masakado's entire family to be traitors and ordered their execution. Two of Masakado's children, Yoshikado and Satsuki hime, somehow managed to escape their execution. They remained in hiding at a temple at the base of Mount Tsukuba for years. Satsuki hime became a devoted nun, but her brother was not interested in religion. He spent his time exploring the mountain and playing at being a samurai.

One day while exploring Mount Tsukuba, Yoshikado encountered a mysterious wizard named Nikushisen. Nikushisen informed Yoshikado that he was the heir of Taira no Masakado, and gave him a magic scroll containing the secrets of frog magic. Yoshikado returned to his sister, and told her everything Nikushisen had said. He gave her the scroll. She studied it and also became a master of frog magic, and took the name Takiyasha hime. The two of them decided to fulfill their father's dream of overthrowing the emperor and ushering in a new order.

In a different version of the story, instead of Yoshikado meeting Nikushisen, Satsuki hime secretly began to perform the dreaded curse ushi no koku mairi—the shrine visit at the hour of the ox. Every night, she snuck into the Kifune Shrine and performed the ritual. After twenty-one nights, she awakened the aramitama—the violent, wicked spirit—of the Kifune Shrine. The aramitama spoke to her, granting her the knowledge of onmyōdō, and instructing her to take the name Takiyasha hime.

Takiyasha hime and Yoshikado returned to their father's fortress of Sōma Castle in Shimōsa Province. They called on the surviving soldiers who remained loyal to their father's cause. Using her newly acquired black magic, Takiyasha hime raised an army of yōkai to continue her father's rebellion against the emperor.

Ōya no Tarō Mitsukuni, a warrior who was knowledgeable about onmyōdō, had heard of Takiyasha hime's plans and set out to Sōma Castle to investigate if the rumors were true. When he arrived, Takiyasha hime disguised herself as a prostitute and tried to seduce Mitsukuni. However, Mitsukuni suspected a trap and told her about the brutal death of Taira no Masakado. She could not contain her emotion, and she fled from Mitsukuni.

That night, Takiyasha hime ambushed Mitsukuni with an army of skeletons and yōkai. She unleashed a gashadokuro upon him—a gigantic skeleton as tall as a castle. Riding into battle on top of a giant toad, Takiyasha hime assaulted the brave warrior Mitsukuni. However, despite her magic, in the end she was defeated. Her short rebellion was snuffed out just as her father's was.

Osakabe hime 長壁姫

TRANSLATION: the lady of the walls
HABITAT: secret areas of Himeji Castle

APPEARANCE: Osakabe hime is a reclusive yōkai who lives high up in the keep of Himeji Castle. She takes the appearance of a majestic old woman wearing a 12-layered kimono.

BEHAVIOR: Osakabe hime is a powerful yōkai, capable of manipulating people like puppets. She is extremely knowledgeable about many things and controls a multitude of *kenzokushin*—animal-like spirits who act as messengers. She can read a person's heart and see their true desires. She can then manipulate them any way she pleases. It is rumored that anybody who sees her face will die instantly.

INTERACTIONS: Osakabe hime absolutely hates meeting people. She spends most of her time hidden away in secret areas of Himeji Castle. However, once a year, she comes out of hiding to meet with the castle lord and foretell the castle's fortune for the next year.

ORIGIN: Osakabe hime's true identity is a mystery. By popular account, she is actually an elderly nine-tailed kitsune who takes the form of this yōkai. According to other accounts, she may be a snake spirit, or the ghost of one of Emperor Fushimi's favorite courtesans. She may even be the sister of Kame hime, a similar yōkai who lived in Inawashiro Castle in Mutsu Province.

Another common legend is that she was originally the kami of the mountain upon which Himeji Castle was built. When Himeji Castle was expanded by Hideyoshi in the 1580s, the shrine dedicated to the local goddess of Mount Hime, Osakabegami, was removed. The goddess was re-enshrined in Harima Sōja, a shrine dedicated to several gods. In the 1600s, when the lord of the castle, Ikeda Terumasa, fell seriously ill, rumors arose that his sickness was due to the goddess's anger at having been removed. In order to appease her, a small temple was built in the keep and Osakabegami was re-enshrined at the top of her mountain. Osakabegami may be the true identity of Osakabe hime.

LEGENDS: During the Edo period, a young page named Morita Zusho went on a dare to go see if a yōkai really lived in the upper floors of Himeji Castle. He waited until nightfall, and then—paper lantern in hand—he climbed to the top of the keep. As brave as he was, Zusho couldn't help imagining what would happen to him if there really was such a creature up there. Finally, when he reached the top floor, he saw a faint light coming from a door in the attic. He peeked in, but whoever was inside had heard him. A woman's voice called out, "Who's there!?"

Zusho was paralyzed with fear. He heard the sound of a kimono rustling. The door opened up to reveal a beautiful, elegant woman in her thirties wearing a splendid 12-layered kimono. Zusho felt his strength return and politely introduced himself and explained his reason for coming.

Amused, the yōkai replied, "A test of bravery, you say? You will need some proof that you actually saw me." She gave him a neck guard of a helmet— piece of his master's own family heirloom armor—to show his master as proof that he met Osakabe hime.

The next day, Zusho told the story of what had happened to his master. Everyone had trouble believing him because they had always heard that the yōkai took the form of an old woman and not a young one. But when Zusho presented the neck guard, his master was shocked and had no choice but to believe the story.

SUGAWARA NO MICHIZANE 菅原道真

APPEARANCE: Sugawara no Michizane was a scholar, poet, and politician who fell out of favor with the emperor and died in exile. He lived from 845 to 903 CE, and is considered one of the greatest scholars and poets in all of Japanese history. After his death, he returned from the grave as a wrathful onryō to wreak his vengeance upon those who had wronged him in life. This earned him a position among the *Nihon San Dai Onryō*—the Three Great Onryō of Japan.

ORIGIN: Sugawara no Michizane was born the eldest son of a high-ranking family of scholars. From a very early age, he showed his brilliance, composing elegant poems by the age of five. He was well-educated and lived a privileged life, gradually climbing the ranks of the bureaucracy and increasing his public standing.

Sugawara no Michizane was an excellent student and scholar. Passing the highest level of government exams at age 26, he received the equivalent of a PhD at age 33. Michizane was selected to be governor of Sanuki Province in 886. During his time as governor he composed a great deal of poetry. In 888, during the Akō Incident, he supported Emperor Uda in his rivalry with Fujiwara no Mototsune. This action earned him a great deal of political clout. When the Emperor consolidated his power, he demoted officials from the Fujiwara clan and promoted officials from the Minamoto clan. Michizane was not a noble, but he too was rewarded. Hs rank rose even further, and he picked up many important court titles, including Ambassador to the Tang Dynasty. This caused unrest among the nobles—particularly the Fujiwaras. They felt indignant that a non-noble scholar should be elevated to such elite ranks.

When Emperor Uda abdicated to Emperor Daigo, Sugawara no Michizane's fortunes declined rapidly. Both Michizane and Fujiwara no Tokihira—the son of Fujiwara no Mototsune, whom Michizane had censured years ago—were the emperor's primary advisors. Tokihira advised the emperor that he should pacify the indignant Fujiwara nobility by sending Michizane away. The emperor listened. Michizane lost his rank and titles, and was demoted from his high position to very minor regional government post at Dazaifu, Chikuzen Province. There, he experienced a thankless life of hard work under much stricter and more severe conditions than in Kyōto.

Despite his humiliation and exile to Kyūshū, Sugawara no Michizane continued to work hard and earnestly for the sake of the country. All the while he prayed for the well-being of the imperial family and the safety of Japan. His hard work was never acknowledged, and he never regained his prestige. He regretted his demotion, and longed for his beloved Kyōto for the rest of his life. Late in the second month of 903, as the plums were blossoming, Michizane died. His heart was filled with loneliness and resentment.

LEGENDS: After Sugawara no Michizane's death, a series of disasters struck Kyōto. Plague and drought spread over the city. His rival Fujiwara no Tokihira died at the age of 39. The sons of Emperor Daigo became sick and died one after another. A lightning bolt struck the Seiryōden palace, causing a fire which killed a number of the officials who had participated in Michizane's demotion and exile. A few months later, Emperor Daigo himself became sick and died. Everyone in the capital had become convinced that Michizane's ghost had become a thunder god and was punishing those who had wronged him.

Sugawara no Michizane's onryō continued to curse the capital with disaster upon disaster. Eventually, the emperor built a shrine to his spirit and posthumously restored his rank and office. He removed any mention of Michizane's exile from the official records. However, it did not appease his spirit, and the disasters kept coming. Finally, in 987, during the reign of Emperor Ichijō, Sugawara no Michizane was promoted and deified as the highest rank of state kami. A special

shrine was built for him in northern Kyōto, and a festival was established in his honor. Michizane became known as Tenman Tenjin, the god of scholarship. The curse was finally appeased.

Tenjin remains a popular god to this day. Paintings of him are hung in homes across the country, and students from all over Japan visit his shrines to pray for luck on their school examinations. Tenjin shrines commonly hold festivals in late February, when plum trees start to bloom, and when school examination results are posted. The plum tree is commonly associated with Tenjin, as it was his favorite tree. Shrines dedicated to him commonly have plum trees on their grounds. Legend has it that while in exile in Dazaifu, he longed so deeply for his favorite plum tree that one night it flew from Kyōto to Kyūshū to be with him. That tree still stands today at the Dazaifu Tenman-gu in Fukuoka.

Sutoku Tennō 崇徳天皇

Translation: Emperor Sutoku

Appearance: Sutoku Tennō is one of the three most famous yōkai to ever haunt Japan. After he died, he transformed—some say into a terrible onryō, some say into a great tengu—and inflicted his wrath upon the imperial court at Kyōto. Along with Tamamo no Mae and Shuten dōji, Emperor Sutoku is one of the legendary *Nihon San Dai Aku Yōkai*—the Three Terrible Yōkai of Japan. Along with Sugawara no Michizane and Taira no Masakado, he is one of the legendary *Nihon San Dai Onryō*—the Three Great Onryō of Japan.

Origin: Prince Akihito was born in 1119 CE, the first son of Emperor Toba. At least that was on the official registry. It was an open secret, known by everyone in the court, that Akihito was actually sired by the retired former Emperor Shirakawa. Akihito was not well liked by his "father," who constantly referred to him as a bastard. His true father Shirakawa may have been the former emperor, but he still wielded considerable power in his retirement. When Prince Akihito was 5 and Emperor Toba was 21, Shirakawa forced Toba into retirement. Akihito became Emperor Sutoku.

After Shirakawa died in 1129, retired Emperor Toba began orchestrating his trap against Emperor Sutoku. He convinced him that the cloistered life of retired emperor was much better than being the actual emperor. He suggested that Sutoku adopt Toba's son Prince Narihito, and retire. In 1142, Sutoku finally did so. Toba oversaw the process, and made sure to record that the emperor was retiring and passing the throne on to Narihito instead of his own progeny. This ensured that Sutoku would wield no power over the young emperor, nor would any future son ever become emperor. The 3-year old Narihito became Emperor Konoe, and the retired Emperor Toba wielded all of the power behind the throne. Toba sent Sutoku's allies to distant provinces, and filled the capital with his own allies. There was nothing Sutoku could do.

Emperor Konoe remained sickly and childless his whole life. He passed away without an heir in 1155 at the age of 17. By this time, Sutoku had his own son. He saw an opportunity to recover his standing. Sutoku and his allies claimed that the throne should pass on to Sutoku's son. Instead the imperial court declared that Toba's fourth son would become Emperor Go-Shirakawa. When Toba died the following year, this dispute escalated into a miniature civil war known as the Hōgen Rebellion. The war was decided in a single battle. The forces of Go-Shirakawa were victorious.

After the Hōgen Rebellion, Go-Shirakawa's forces were merciless. Those who fought against the emperor were executed, along with their entire families. Former Emperor Sutoku was banished from Kyōto and forced to spend the rest of his days exiled to Sanuki Province. He shaved his head and became a monk, devoting himself copying holy manuscripts to send back to Kyōto. The court feared that the deposed Sutoku would attempt to curse them. It was rumored that he had bitten off his own tongue and wrote the manuscripts in his own blood, imbuing them with his hatred for the merciless imperial court. The court added insult to injury by refusing to accept any of his manuscripts.

In 1164, Sutoku passed away, defeated, deposed, and humiliated—and most importantly full of rage for the imperial court. When news of his death reached Emperor Go-Shirakawa, the emperor ignored it. He ordered that nobody should go into mourning, and that no state funeral would be held for such a criminal.

Legends: After his death, strange things began to happen. Sutoku's body was set aside while its caretakers awaited funeral instructions from the emperor. After 20 days, his body was still as fresh as it had been on the day he died. While his coffin was taken to be cremated, a terrible storm rolled

in. The caretakers placed the casket on the ground to take shelter. After the storm passed, the stones around the casket were soaked with fresh blood. When his body was finally cremated, the ashes descended upon Kyōto in a dark cloud.

Afterwards, for many years, disaster upon disaster struck the capital. Go-Shirakawa's successor, Emperor Nijo, died suddenly at age 23. Storms, plagues, fires, droughts, and earthquakes all pounded the capital. Imperial power weakened. Clan rivalries set into motion by the Hōgen Rebellion escalated. Many of Go-Shirakawa's allies were killed in battles, and the country stepped closer and closer to all-out civil war. In 1180, the Genpei War broke out. In 5 bloody years, the power of the imperial court had vanished, and the Kamakura shogunate took over Japan. All of this was attributed to Emperor Sutoku's vengeance.

Sutoku finally returned to the capital during the Meiji era. In 1868, he was enshrined as a kami in the Shiramine Shrine in Kyōto. The Takaya Shrine in Kagawa also enshrines one of the stones onto which Sutoku's blood flowed during the rainstorm before his cremation. Despite this, there are still rumors that his curse might still linger. In 2012, when NHK broadcast the drama *Taira no Kiyomori*, an earthquake struck the Kanto region right at the moment when Emperor Sutoku transformed into an onryō.

TAMAMO NO MAE 玉藻前

TRANSLATION: a nickname literally meaning "Lady Duckweed"

APPEARANCE: Tamamo no Mae is one of the most famous kitsune in Japanese mythology. A nine-tailed magical fox, she is also one of the most powerful yōkai that has ever lived. Her magical abilities were matched only by her trickiness and lust for power. Tamamo no Mae lived during the Heian period, and though she may not have succeeded in her plan to kill the emperor and take his place, her actions destabilized the country and lead it towards one of the most important civil wars in Japanese history. For that reason, Tamamo no Mae is considered one of the *Nihon San Dai Aku Yōkai*—the Three Terrible Yōkai of Japan.

ORIGIN: Tamamo no Mae appears in numerous texts and has been a popular subject throughout Japanese history. Her story is portrayed in literature, noh, kabuki, bunraku, and other forms of art. There are several variations on her story.

LEGENDS: Tamamo no Mae was born some 3,500 years ago in what is now China. Her early life is a mystery, but she eventually became a powerful sorceress. After hundreds of more years she became a white faced, golden furred kyūbi no kitsune—a nine-tailed fox with supreme magical power. In addition, she was an expert at manipulation. She used her charms and wit to advance her standing and influence world affairs.

During the Shang Dynasty Tamamo no Mae was known as Daji. She disguised herself as a beautiful woman and became the favorite concubine of King Zhou of Shang. Daji was a model of human depravity. She held orgies in the palace gardens. Her fondness for watching and inventing new forms of torture are legendary. Daji eventually brought about the fall of the entire Shang Dynasty. She managed to escape execution, and fled to the Magadha kingdom in India in 1046 BCE.

In Magadha, she was known as Lady Kayō, and became a consort of King Kalmashapada, known in Japan as Hanzoku. She used her beauty and charms to dominate the king, causing him to devour children, murder priests, and commit other unspeakable horrors. Eventually—whether because she ran out children to eat or because Kalmashapada began to turn away from her and towards Buddhism—she fled back to China.

During the Zhou Dynasty she called herself Bao Si, and was known as one of the most desirable women in all of China. In 779 BCE she became a concubine of King You. Not satisfied as just a mistress, she manipulated the king into deposing his wife Queen Shen and making Bao Si his new queen. Though she was beautiful, Bao Si rarely ever smiled. In order to please his beautiful new wife, King You committed acts of such evil and atrocity that eventually all of his nobles abandoned and betrayed him. Eventually, King You was killed and Bao Si captured and the Western Zhou Dynasty was brought to an end in 771 BCE. Somehow Bao Si managed to escape again; she went into hiding for many years.

Little is known of her activities until the 700s, when she resurfaced disguised as a 16-year old girl named Wakamo. She tricked the leaders of the 10th Japanese envoy to the Tang Dynasty—Kibi no Makibi, Abe no Nakamaro, and Ganjin—as they were preparing to return home to Japan. Wakamo joined their crew and took the ship to Japan, where she hid herself away for over 300 years.

In the 1090s, she resurfaced once again. This time she transformed herself into a human baby and hid by the side of the road. A married couple found the baby and rescued it, taking her in as their daughter and naming her Mikuzume (sometimes spell Mizukume). She proved to be an

exceedingly intelligent and talented young girl, and was so beautiful that she attracted to attention of everyone around her. When she was 7 years old, Mikuzume recited poetry before the emperor. His imperial majesty immediately took a liking to her and employed her as a servant in his court.

Mikuzume excelled at court, absorbing knowledge like a sponge. There was no question she could not answer, whether it was about music, history, astronomy, religion, or Chinese classics. Her clothes were always clean and unwrinkled. She always smelled pleasant. Mikuzume had the most beautiful face in all of Japan, and everyone who saw her loved her.

During the summer of her 18th year, a poetry and instrument recital was held in Mikuzume's honor. During the recital, an unexpected storm fell upon the palace. All of the candles in the recital room were snuffed, leaving the participants in the dark. Suddenly, a bright light emanated from Mikuzume's body, illuminating the room. Everybody at court was so impressed by her genius and declared that she must have had an exceedingly good and holy previous life. She was given the name Tamamo no Mae. Emperor Toba, already exceedingly fond of her, made her his consort.

Almost immediately after she became the emperor's consort, the emperor fell deathly ill. None of the court physicians could determine the cause, and so the onmyōji Abe no Yasunari was called in. Abe no Yasunari read the emperor's fortune and divined that he was marked by a bad omen. After that, the highest priests and monks were summoned to the palace to pray for the emperor's health.

The best prayers of the highest priests had no effect, however. The emperor continued to grow worse. Abe no Yasunari was summoned again to read the emperor's fortune. This time, to his horror the onmyōji discovered that the emperor's beloved Tamamo no Mae was the cause of his illness. She was a kitsune in disguise, and was shortening the emperor's life span in order to take over as ruler of Japan. Emperor Toba was reluctant to believe the diviner's words, but agreed to test Tamamo no Mae just to be sure.

To save the emperor's life, Abe no Yasunari prepared the Taizan Fukun no Sai, the most secret and most powerful spell known to onmyōdō. Tamamo no Mae was ordered to perform part of the ritual. They reasoned that an evil spirit would not be able to participate in such a holy ritual. Though she was reluctant to participate, the emperor's ministers persuaded her. They told her that it would increase her standing an admiration among the court. She had little choice but to accept.

When the ritual was performed, Tamamo no Mae dressed even more beautifully than normal. She recited the holy worlds as expected and played her part extremely well. But just as she prepared to wave the ceremonial staff, she vanished. Abe no Yasunari's divination was confirmed. The court flew into an uproar.

Soon after, word arrived that women and children were disappearing near Nasuno in Shimotsuke Province. The court sorcerers determined that Tamamo no Mae was the cause, and it was decided that she must be destroyed once and for all. The emperor summoned the best warriors in all of the land and then charged the most superb of them, Kazusanosuke and Miuranosuke, to find Tamamo no Mae. The warriors gladly accepted the honor. They purified themselves and set out with an army of 80,000 men to slay the nine-tailed kitsune.

Upon reaching Nasuno the army quickly found the kitsune. The warriors chased her for days and days, but the fox used her magical powers and outsmarted them time and time again, easily escaping. The army grew weary, and frustration set in. It seemed that nothing they did was working. However, Kazusanosuke and Miuranosuke would not accept the shame of defeat and vowed to press on. They practiced harder, honing their tactics, and eventually picked up the kitsune's trail.

One night, Miuranosuke had a prophetic dream. A beautiful young girl appeared before him, crying. She begged: "Tomorrow I will lose my life to you. Please save me." Miuranosuke adamantly refused, and upon waking the warriors set out again to find Tamamo no Mae. Sure enough, the next day they caught her. Miuranosuke fired two arrows, one through the fox's flank and one through its neck. Kazusanosuke swung his blade. It was over, just as the dream had said.

However, Tamamo no Mae's evil did not end with her death. One year after she died, Emperor Konoe died, heirless. The following year, her lover and former Emperor Toba died as well. A succession crisis ignited between forces loyal to Emperor Go-Shirakawa and forces loyal to former Emperor Sutoku. This crisis started the Fujiwara-Minamoto rivalry that led to the Genpei War, the end of the Heian period, and the rise of the first shoguns. As if that were not enough, Tamamo no Mae's spirit haunted a massive boulder which killed every living thing that touched it.

SESSHŌ SEKI 殺生石

TRANSLATION: killing stone

APPEARANCE: Sesshō seki is a large boulder that stands in the plains of Nasuno, Shimotsuke (modern day Tochigi Prefecture). Around it is a desolate, lifeless field, filled with toxic gasses and the skeletons of animals who strayed too near.

ORIGIN: Sesshō seki was formed when the evil nine-tailed kitsune Tamamo no Mae was slain. Her hunters returned triumphantly, bearing her body to the capital. Her spirit, however, attached itself to a large boulder near where she fell. It continued to kill long after her death. Any living thing that wandered close enough to the stone died instantly. Sesshō seki remained a deadly landmark until 1385 CE, when Tamamo no Mae's spirit was put to rest once and for all.

LEGENDS: One day, a high priest named Gennō was traveling through Shimotsuke Province when he noticed a peculiar sight—the birds in the air fell to their deaths whenever they passed over a certain boulder in the plain of Nasuno. At the base of the stone was a pile of dead birds. Gennō wondered what could cause such a phenomenon. Not long afterwards, a local woman appeared near the priest, and he asked her about the stone.

The woman explained that Sesshō seki was haunted by the spirit of Tamamo no Mae. She told him the story of the fox courtesan, and then vanished. Gennō realized that the woman had been the ghost of the infamous kitsune. He performed a Buddhist memorial service over the stone, and suddenly Tamamo no Mae's spirit reappeared and confessed all of her sins, going back thousands of years all the way to India and China. After hearing Gennō's pure words and Buddhist teachings, Tamamo no Mae repented all of her evils and swore never again to do wrong, and then disappeared. Her spirit, exorcised from the rock, never harmed anyone again.

Gennō—whose name means hammer—hit the rock and it burst into many pieces. The pieces flew all across Japan, where many of them remain today. The base of the rock still stands in Nasu, Tochigi. Other chunks flew to Okayama, Niigata, Hiroshima, and Ōita where they were enshrined. Smaller fragments landed in present-day Fukui, Gifu, Nagano, Gunma, and parts of Shikoku, where they were picked up and used as magical amulets to perform charms or curses.

SHIKIGAMI 式神

TRANSLATION: ceremonial spirit
ALTERNATE NAMES: shikijin, shiki no kami
DIET: varies

APPEARANCE: Shikigami are servant spirits used by onmyōji in rituals for various purposes. Some are used as charms for good fortune, some are used as amulets for protection, and some are used as curses. To call a shikigami means to call a god, a demon, a yōkai, or a ghost and to utilize its power for some deed or another.

INTERACTIONS: Shikigami can be powerful and dangerous. They come in many forms. The most common are enshrined in small objects, such as strips of paper or amulets. Others may come in the form of animal possessions, using the bodies of chickens, cows, or dogs as vessels. The most dreadful shikigami take the form of humans, ghosts, yōkai, or oni.

While shikigami are powerful and terrifying, perhaps their most horrifying aspect is that they never act under their own will; they are slaves in the service of human magic users who tell them what to do.

CONTROLLING SPIRITS

According to Shinto belief, humans and kami all have a soul known as *mitama*. A mitama is divided into four separate spirits, or *tamashii*, which oppose each other. These are controlled by another spirit, calling a *naohi*, which forms a connection between heaven and earth.

The four tamashii are *aramitama*, *nigimitama*, *sakimitama*, and *kushimitama*. Aramitama is the spirit of courage, perseverance, and extroversion. Nigimitama is the spirit of peace, harmony, and cooperation. Sakimitama is the spirit of happiness, love, and affection. Kushimitama is the spirit of wisdom, observation, and analysis. Aramitama and nigimitama oppose each other, while sakimitama and kushimitama are considered to be aspects of the nigimitama. All four of these spirits are controlled by the naohi—the oversoul—and they work together to form one soul.

When dealing with spirit summoning, it is important to know which tamashii you are dealing with. Nigimitama manifest as benevolent and helpful spirits. Aramitama manifest as raging, wild, dangerous spirits. These opposing tamashii differ so much—even within the same kami—that they can seem to be two separate beings. Much of Shinto is based on the concept of pacifying the aggressive aramitama and bringing forth the peaceful nigimitama.

Helpful prayers and songs are normally directed to the nigimitama of the kami in order to bring out its benevolence. Dark summoning and spells meant to harm others invoke the much more dangerous aramitama.

Tanuki tsuki 狸憑き

TRANSLATION: tanuki (raccoon dog) possession

APPEARANCE: Spirit possession can be caused by humans and ghosts, but frequently it is the work of animals with supernatural powers. One of the most common animal possessions is called tanuki tsuki—possession by tanuki spirits.

INTERACTIONS: When tanuki possess human beings, their victims develop strange new personality traits. One of the most common changes is gluttony. Victims become intensely hungry and eat and eat, even going so far as to eat spoiled and ruined food. Although possessed humans grow vast waists from this gluttony, all of the nutrition goes to the tanuki spirits. Victims only grow weaker and weaker until finally they die from malnutrition. Other common symptoms of tanuki possession include unexplained illness, melancholy, becoming overly talkative, sudden outbursts of violence, or abnormally increased libido.

Tanuki possess humans for various reasons, but common ones include revenge for destroying the tanuki's den, or simply just as a prank. In rare cases, some human families have harnessed the power of animal possession for their own use. Some legends tell of people offering food to old, wild tanuki, taming them, and then using their spirits to possess their enemies.

Because tanuki are powerful yōkai, it is difficult to escape tanuki tsuki. Either the tanuki must leave of its own will, or it must be driven out by a powerful yamabushi, priest, or onmyōji. Another solution is to deify the tanuki. A tanuki elevated to the level of a kami will no longer possess humans. Many villages—particularly in Shikoku—have built shrines to worship particularly troublesome tanuki.

KEEPING IT IN THE FAMILY

Animals and spirits that can possess humans are called *tsukimono*. Some families, called *tsukimono suji*, keep animal spirits as servants. They are able to use them as shikigami. These servant spirits are called upon to perform wicked deeds against the family's enemies. Often these families retain control over their tsukimono for generations, passing them on down the family line like precious heirlooms. The use of tsukimono black magic against others has been illegal since long ago. Those with the power carefully guard their secrets.

Common animals used by tsukimono suji families are dogs, such as inugami, various types of foxes, snakes, weasels, and martens. Tanuki are less commonly used in this way, but the use of tanuki spirits by humans is not unheard of. Owning a tsukimono allowed a family to gain power and money. Many became nouveaux riche. They were envied for their wealth but feared for their taboo powers. People were strongly advised against marrying into tsukimono suji families.

Inugami 犬神

TRANSLATION: dog god, dog spirit
ALTERNATE NAMES: ingame, irigami

APPEARANCE: Inugami are a kind of shikigami that was once popular in Kyūshū, Shikoku, and elsewhere in western Japan. In public, inugami look identical to ordinary dogs. This disguise lets them blend in with society. However, their true form is a desiccated, mummified dog's head, often dressed up in ceremonial trappings. This is used as a fetish to summon and control the spirit. This is kept safe and away from prying eyes, usually in a secret shrine in its owner's house.

INTERACTIONS: Inugami are used for all manner of nefarious deeds. They serve their masters loyally, performing tasks just like trained, faithful dogs. They are bound to one person or one family only, and unless seriously mistreated they remain loyal forever. They can even be inherited from generation to generation like heirlooms.

Like other shikigami, inugami are powerful spirits. Their primary use is to possess and control other people. They are created from strong emotions, and thus are skilled at possessing emotionally unstable or weak people.

Not only humans, but animals such as cows and horses, and even inanimate objects, can be possessed by inugami. Possessed animals become sick and unable to work. Possessed tools become dull, or are otherwise rendered completely unusable.

People who find themselves possessed by an inugami are in for some serious misfortune. Inugami usually enter through the ears and settle in the internal organs. Signs of inugami possession include chest pain, pain in the hands, feet, or shoulders, feelings of deep jealousy, and suddenly barking like a dog. Some victims develop intense hunger and turn into gluttons. It is said that people who die while possessed by an inugami are found with markings all over their body resembling the teeth and claw marks of a dog.

The only way to be cured of inugami tsuki is to hire an onmyōji to expel the spirit. This could take a very, very long time and involve a great deal of money.

The technique for creating inugami is passed down along bloodlines. Such families are known as *inugami mochi.* These families keep their inugami hidden in the back rooms of their houses, under their beds, in dressers, or hidden among water jars. Inugami mochi families own as many inugami as there are members of the household. When a new person joins the family, they receive their own familiar.

Inugami are treated like family members by inugami mochi households. Most of the time these dog spirits do their master's bidding without complaint. However, like living dogs, occasionally a resentful inugami might betray an owner that has grown too abusive or domineering. Inugami can turn on these brutal masters and savagely bite them to death.

While inugami are used to bring wealth and prosperity to their families, occasionally they might cause a household to fall into ruin. Practicing this sort of black magic was illegal and frowned upon (although that didn't stop the aristocracy from dabbling in onmyōdō sorcery). If an inugami mochi family member was even suspected of cursing another family, the accused would be forced to apologize and leave their estates to live on the outskirts of town, secluded from family, friends, and the comfortable aristocratic life. Even if the victims were eventually cured of their possession, the accused and all of their offspring for generations to follow had to maintain a solitary lifestyle. They were outcast from the rest of society, and viewed by others as wicked and tainted.

ORIGIN: No one knows when or where the practice of creating inugami begun. There is evidence of an ancient tradition of inugami worship stretching from western Japan down to Okinawa. By the Heian period, some 1000 years ago, at the height of classical Japanese civilization, the use of animal spirits as tools of sorcery had been outlawed.

How to Make an Inugami

The process to make an inugami is particularly brutal. First, you starve a dog by chaining it up just out of reach of some food, or else burying it up to its neck. In time, the dog will go berserk out of hunger. At the moment of its greatest desperation, as it strains with all its might to reach the food, you chop the dog's head off. This traps the intense emotions in the skull. Then, you bury the severed head in a busy street—usually a crossroads where many people walk. The trampling of hundreds or thousands of people over the buried head adds stress and causes the trapped emotions to transform the dog's spirit into an onryō. (Occasionally these severed heads escape and fly about, chasing after food, animated by the power of the dog's hunger and rage. When this happens, either the head has to be captured or the process begun anew.) Eventually the head is dug up from the crossroads, baked or dried, and then enshrined in a bowl. It is now an inugami. The enshrined spirit will do whatever it is commanded for the rest of time.

KANASHIBARI 金縛り

TRANSLATION: bound up with iron

APPEARANCE: Kanashibari is the Japanese term for sleep paralysis, a phenomenon when REM sleep overlaps with waking consciousness. Victims' bodies are still paralyzed in sleep, but eyes are open and the mind is half-awake—the real and dream worlds mix together. Stories about kanashibari go back to ancient times. The phenomenon was attributed to supernatural forces acting on the body. There are many legends about kanashibari, and each one points to a different cause.

ORIGIN: The most common form of kanashibari comes from spirit possession. When a person is possessed by inugami, kitsune, tanuki, or other kinds of tsukimono, one of the possible symptoms they can develop is immobility or sleep paralysis. This could sometimes be overcome if a shugenja recited Buddhist sutras to drive out the possessing animal spirit. Once the spirit was driven out, the kanashibari would disappear, and all would be well again.

Other kinds of yōkai can inflict kanashibari as well. House-haunting yōkai, such as makuragaeshi, are frequent culprits. Victims wake up in the middle of the night, feeling a crushing weight on their chest, and often see the ghost of a small child or some monster sitting on top of them. This can occur sporadically, or even every night, depending on the nature of the yōkai involved. Though not actually harmful, it is a terrifying experience for the victim.

Kanashibari can even be caused by humans—usually by priests or onmyōji invoking the gods. The tale of Kiyo hime features one passage where the jealous princess is chasing after her lover, Anchin. Trying to escape her advances, the Anchin asks the gods of the Kumano Shrine for help. They are able to trap Kiyo hime in kanashibari, giving Anchin time to flee.

Finally, kanashibari can be caused by ghosts—ikiryō or shiryō. There are many variations, but this famous account from a popular ghost story in Iwate Prefecture (old Mutsu Province) is fairly typical: during the middle of the night, a man woke up with an ominous, foreboding sense of dread. He realized that he couldn't move, even though he was wide awake. It felt as if powerful arms were gripping him tight, keeping him immobile. Suddenly, an invisible force tugged on his legs and dragged him out from under his futon and towards the door! After a desperate struggle, he finally snapped out of the sleep paralysis, and saw the ghost of a middle aged woman rise up into the ceiling.

Katashiro 形代

TRANSLATION: form substitution

APPEARANCE: Katashiro are human-shaped dolls. They are usually made of paper, but sometimes of wood, straw, or metal. There are different shapes and designs of katashiro to suit the many purposes they serve.

INTERACTIONS: Katashiro are a type of *yorishiro*—ceremonial objects used as a substitution for someone or something. Specifically they are used as a substitution for a person during a ritual. They are commonly used in purification rituals, where a person's sins are transferred into the katashiro. The karashiro is then discarded into a river or body of water, taking the sin away with it.

Katashiro are also frequently used to ward off evil in a similar fashion. If you are suffering bad luck, a katashiro can be used to absorb the bad luck from you or prevent bad things from occurring. If you suspect that you are going to be targeted by a curse, a katashiro can be prepared as a substitute target for your person. The doll will receive all of the evil effects in place of the intended target.

Katashiro can even be used in spells or curses as a substitution for a real human target. Usually this involves inscribing the name, birthdate, and other personal information on the paper doll. The spell is performed on the doll, after which the intended effects happen to the actual person.

WARA NINGYŌ 藁人形

TRANSLATION: straw doll
ALTERNATE NAMES: suge ningyō (sedge doll)

APPEARANCE: Wara ningyō are a popular kind of katashiro made of straw. Wara ningyō most commonly depict humans, but they are occasionally made in the shape of horses or other animals too.

INTERACTIONS: Wara ningyō are used extensively as wards against evil. During the Heian period, wara ningyō would be placed along the sides of the roads for protection against plague. It was hoped that the evil spirits which brought disease would nest in the straw bodies instead of living human bodies. Afterwards, the straw dolls would be discarded into a river, which would also purify the evil spirits.

Wara ningyō are popular devices in a number of dark rituals. They are combined with something from the recipient of the curse, such as a piece of hair. This transforms the doll into a substitute for the intended target. Long nails are pushed through the wara ningyō, harming the subject as well as the doll.

There are specific rules for creating different types of wara ningyō. These detail the materials to be used, the way the dolls are constructed, and the objects to be inserted into them. It can be difficult to find the materials needed to perform curses. The required items are not sold in most stores. However, some websites sell premade curse kits that contain all of the items you might need to perform a specific curse, including a wara ningyō, long nails, a mallet, pre-written curses with blanks for the recipient's name, and other accessories. Of course, performing such rituals is illegal.

271

HITOBASHIRA 人柱

TRANSLATION: human pillar
HABITAT: found in bridges, castles, dams, and other large constructions

APPEARANCE: Hitobashira refers to the gruesome practice of burying a living human being in the foundations of important buildings—bridges, dams, tunnels, and particularly castles. It was a common practice during large construction projects from ancient times through the 16th century. However there is evidence that hitobashira were still being used in some construction projects during the 20th century.

BEHAVIOR: This form of sacrifice was used as a magical ward for the building being constructed. It was believed that the sacrifice of a human soul would appease the nature spirits in an area—particularly the river spirits in areas where flooding was common. They were also used to ward castles against assault, fire, and other disasters both man-made and natural.

ORIGIN: Although hitobashira literally means human pillar, the actual meaning is more complicated. Pillars and Shinto have a long relationship—kami can be enshrined in pillar-like sacred trees, the oldest shrines were built upon pillars, and hashira, in addition to meaning pillar, is also used as the *josūshi*—Japanese counter word—for kami. The *bashira* in hitobashira refers not to a literal pillar, but actually to this counter word. The human was enshrined in a manner similar to a kami of the building to which he or she was sacrificed, becoming both a literal pillar and a connection to the gods. Very often, small stone memorials were erected in honor of the hitobashira who were sacrificed to a building. Some still stand today.

LEGENDS: A few famous castles in Japan are connected to legends of hitobashira. Maruoka Castle in Fukui Prefecture (old Echizen Province), one of the oldest surviving castles in Japan, is said to contain a hitobashira in the central pillar of the keep.

While Maruoka Castle was being constructed, its walls kept collapsing no matter how many times they were repaired. It was decided that a person should be sacrificed and made into a hitobashira in order to improve the stability of the castle. A poor, one-eyed woman named Oshizu was selected for the honor of becoming a hitobashira. As a reward for her sacrifice, she was promised that her son would be made a samurai. After she was sacrificed the castle was completed. However, before her son could be made a samurai, the castle's lord was transferred to another province, and the promise was left unkept.

Every year thereafter, the castle's moat overflowed when the heavy spring rains came. The people of Maruoka blamed this on Oshizu's vengeance, and called this rain "tears of Oshizu's sorrow." Afterwards, a cenotaph was erected for Oshizu inside the castle grounds to calm her spirit.

Ichijama 生邪魔

TRANSLATION: living evil spirit
ALTERNATE NAMES: ichimabui, ikimaburi
HABITAT: Okinawa and islands in southern Kyūshū

APPEARANCE: Ichijama is a curse from Okinawa. It is a type of ikiryō—a spirit of a still-living person which leaves the body to haunt its victim. The magic which summons this spirit, the person who casts the spell, and the family line of that person are all referred to as ichijama. Not only people, but cows, pigs, horses and other livestock, as well as crops can be cursed by an ichijama.

INTERACTIONS: An ichijama is summoned by praying to a special doll known as an *ichijama butokii*. The ichijama butokii is boiled in a pot while reciting the name of the body part which is to be cursed. After the ritual is performed, a spirit which looks exactly like the person casting the spell visits the home of the intended victim. It delivers a gift to its target—usually fruit or vegetables such as bananas, garlic, or wild onions. After receiving the gift, the target develops an unidentifiable sickness in whichever body part was chanted during the spell. If untreated, the victim will die.

Omyōdō did not exist in Okinawa, so this curse could only be overcome with the help of Okinawan magic, by shamans known as yuta. This was accomplished by performing yet another curse. The yuta would bind the victim's thumbs together and hit them with a nail while chanting bad things about the curse victim. Performing this curse would drive out the ichijama from its victim.

ORIGIN: The ability to summon an ichijama is a hereditary secret passed down from mother to daughter. Families with such magical power are said to be very beautiful and have a sharp look in their eyes. The ability to use black magic carries a strong social stigma in Okinawa. Marrying into one of these families should be avoided at all costs. But it is difficult to tell; ichijama clans are often careful about hiding their family secret.

Ushi no koku mairi 丑の刻参り

TRANSLATION: shrine visit at the hour of the ox
ALTERNATE NAMES: ushi no toki mairi

APPEARANCE: Ushi no koku mairi is one of the most famous and dreaded black magic spells. It takes place between 1:00 and 3:00 in the morning, during the hour of the ox. This is the period of darkest night, when the border between the world of the living and the world of the dead is weakest. During this hour, evil spirits are at their greatest power.

INTERACTIONS: There are a number of complicated steps required to perform this curse ritual, and they vary from account to account. In general, you must first construct a wara ningyō containing a small piece of the intended target's body—a piece of hair, blood, fingernails, or skin, for example. Alternatively, you may use an image of their target, or a piece of paper with the target's name written on it. Then, you put on the ceremonial dress—a white kimono and obi, with thick white face powder. An upturned trivet is placed on your head, and you attach tapers to its legs and light them. Tall, single-toothed geta are worn on your feet. A mirror is carried over your breast, a dagger is tucked behind the obi, and a comb is held between your teeth.

Thus prepared, you must sneak into a shrine during the hour of the ox and approach the shrine's sacred tree. Then, you hammer a long iron nail through the wara ningyō into the tree— symbolically breaking the barrier between the world of the living and the spirit world. You call out to evil spirits, demons, and yōkai to come into the world. This ritual must be repeated every night for many nights, and it is very important that the person performing the curse not be seen. If there are any witnesses, they must be killed immediately. Otherwise the evil of this curse will rebound onto the caster.

Once the ritual is completed, something—it is not clear what—terrible happens. According to some accounts, the curse victim dies an agonizing death upon completion of the ritual. In other accounts, the entire process is torture for the victim, causing days of suffering while the curse is being performed. In some stories, the curse summons yōkai which haunt the victim, and in other stories, the person performing the ritual transforms into a powerful oni or kijo.

LEGENDS: A few shrines are well-known for this sort of black magic. Kifune Shrine and Jishu Shrine in Kyōto, and Ikurei Shrine in Okayama Prefecture (old Bitchū Province) are the most famous ones. In the old days, these were popular locations for jealous lovers to perform this curse. Even today, every now and then, shrine officials find wara ningyō hammered into trees at these shrines.

Taizan Fukun no Sai 泰山府君祭

TRANSLATION: the Taizan Fukun (Lord Taizan) ceremony

APPEARANCE: Taizan Fukun no Sai is one of the most secret and powerful onmyōdō rituals. It is jealously guarded by the few who know it, and strongly coveted by those who don't.

ORIGIN: This spell was developed in ancient China by Taoist philosophers. It is named for Lord Taizan, the god of the mountain Taishan in Shandong, China and one of the kings of hell. He is one of the most important deities in Onmyōdō. In this ritual, the supplicant beseeches Lord Taizan, Great King Enma, and the other judges of Meido and Jigoku to lengthen a person's life span, save someone from death, or even restore life to the dead. Gold, silver, silk, saddled horses, and human life—usually substitutes in the form of katashiro, or paper dolls—are offered to the gods. No mantras or magical worlds are spoken; the gods are simply invited to sit down and participate. A formal letter of request is read to them, detailing the offerings and the virtues of the supplicants, and the precise divine intervention desired.

The Abe clan was famous for their knowledge of this spell. It is one of the reasons they were able to maintain a monopoly on the imperial Bureau of Onmyōdō. Under their offices, this spell was routinely performed for the emperors in order to increase their life spans and protect the country.

LEGENDS: Abe no Seimei is particularly famous for his use of Taizan Fukun no Sai. He resurrected his father, who was murdered by Ashiya Dōman, and used it many other times in the service of the emperor and country.

Once, a high ranking monk of Mii-dera known as Chikō fell gravely ill. It was determined that his illness was the result of karma, and thus could not be cured with medicine. Abe no Seimei was summoned. He divined Chikō's fortune, and discovered that death was imminent. However, Abe no Seimei said that if someone was willing to trade life spans with Chikō, he could perform the Taizan Fukun no Sai and save the priest's life.

The priests all looked at each other uncomfortably. As much as they loved and admired Chikō, nobody was willing to sacrifice his own life in order to save him. Finally, a young man named Shōkū—an average pupil who had been studying for many years yet had never attracted the attention of Chikō or the other teachers—stepped forward and offered his own life.

Abe no Seimei accepted the offer. He immediately performed the Taizan Fukun no Sai. Shōkū writhed in anguish, his life span shrinking away, while Chikō rapidly began to recover. Finally, Chikō was cured, and Shōkū lay on death's door. As the young pupil's last breath left his body, he prayed with all his heart to a nearby painting of Fudō Myōō. Just then, tears poured from the painted eyes of Fudō Myōō, and the god's voice was heard:

"If you would take the place of your teacher, then let me take your place instead."

Suddenly, Shōkū and Chikō sat up, both of then restored to life.

HINODE 日の出

TRANSLATION: sunrise

APPEARANCE: Hinode, the break of dawn, signals the end of the power of evil spirits over the waking world. The holy light of the sun banishes yōkai, ghosts, and demons back to the places from which they came. As the morning light fills the shadows, unknown things no longer lurk. As the sun's rays pierce the dark forests, strange shapes no longer hide among the trees. The time of meeting evil spirits is over. Once again the world is safe for humans.

ORIGIN: The sun has always been a central part of Japanese religion. Amaterasu, the sun goddess, is the most important deity in Shinto and is worshipped across Japan. The importance of the sun in Japanese culture can be seen in Japan's nickname—the land of the rising sun—on the Japanese flag, and in the native word for Japan itself: *Nihon*, "the origin of the sun."

In Japanese artwork, the sun often appears as the final scene in picture scrolls depicting yōkai and the night parade of one hundred demons. Similarly, Toriyama Sekien's second illustrated yōkai encyclopedia, *Konjaku Gazu Zoku Hyakki*, opens with ōmagatoki and closes with hinode, depicting the monsters that rule the world from dusk until dawn.

ACKNOWLEDGMENTS

When I first started writing about and painting yōkai years ago, I had no idea that the world was on the verge of a major yōkai boom. In the few years since the publication of my first book, *The Night Parade of One Hundred Demons*, it seems like yōkai has become a household word. What started as an obscure interest for me many years ago has blown up into a huge phenomenon, and I feel so lucky to be a small part of the yōkai fandom which has swept the world.

Like with *Night Parade*, all of the funding for *The Hour of Meeting Evil Spirits* was raised online through Kickstarter. I am so grateful to all of my fans who returned to back me again for my second book, as well as all of the new fans who took a chance on me and decided to give me their support. The second time around was no less exhilarating than the first. I consider myself extremely lucky to have fans who are so interested in and enthusiastic about my work. Just as with my first book, *The Hour of Meeting Evil Spirits* could not have been made without all of your questions, comments, and support

This book was created using free and open source software. The illustrations were painted in GIMP, the text was written in LibreOffice, the book layout and design were done in Scribus, and all of this was done on the Ubuntu operating system. The free typefaces used in this book are The Fell Types for English and Iwata Gyōsho (イワタ行書) for Japanese. The hard work and generosity of those who make free open-source software makes it possible for small authors and artists like me to publish. Without them, this book could not have been made.

My primary source for the information in this book has been the work of Edo period artist Toriyama Sekien. His works and those of other Edo period yōkai artists who served as a my sources can be found in Wikimedia Commons and other online databases, such as the one maintained by The International Research Center for Japanese Studies. The yōkai research done by Kenji Murakami and Shigeru Mizuki played an important part in filling in the gaps left by earlier yōkai researchers. Finally, a large amount of information came out of traveling around Japan and listening to the various yōkai stories people were willing to share with me. I will always be grateful to these people for sharing a part of their culture with me.

Lastly, I owe a great deal to my wife, who has served as a partner to my in creating this book just as she did with my first book. She helped me with the least exciting parts of research for this book: deciphering scrolls written in archaic Japanese, contacting yōkai experts in Japan to clarify nitpicky details and answer difficult questions, and hunting down obscure documents to find information on some of the rarest and weirdest yōkai. I never could have finished all of the research required for this book without her help.

It was always my hope to create a second yōkai volume after *Night Parade*. It seemed like the more research I did, the more new yōkai I learned about. Before my first book was finished, I had already logged enough yōkai to write a second book. Now that this book is done I have enough to write at least a third and a fourth. As long as people remain interested, I hope to keep painting and writing about yōkai. To all of you who helped make *The Hour of Meeting Evil Spirits* into a reality, I am truly grateful.

Yōkai References and Further Reading

Books

Foster, Michael Dylan. *The Book of Yokai: Mysterious Creatures of Japanese Folklore*. Los Angeles: University of California Press, 2015.

Kyogoku, Natsuhiko. *Yōkai zukan*. Tōkyō: Kokusho Kankōkai, 2000.

Mizuki, Shigeru. *Mujara*. Tōkyō: Softgarage Inc., 2008.

Murakami, Kenji. *Yōkai jiten*. Tōkyō: Mainichi Newspaper Co. Ltd, 2000.

Tada, Katsumi. *Edo yōkai karuta*. Tōkyō: Kokusho Kankōkai, 1998.

Toriyama, Sekien. *Toriyama Sekien gazu hyakki yagyō zen gashū*. Tōkyō: Kadokawa Shoten Publishing Co., 2005.

Yumoto, Koichi. *Yokai Museum: The Art of Japanese Supernatural Beings from YUMOTO Koichi Collection*. Tōkyō: PIE Books, 2013.

Online

Database of Images of Strange Phenomena and Yōkai. International Research Center for Japanese Studies. <http://www.nichibun.ac.jp/YoukaiGazouMenu/>.

Folktale Data of Strange Phenomena and Yōkai. International Research Center for Japanese Studies. <http://www.nichibun.ac.jp/YoukaiDB/>.

Hyakumonogatari Kaidankai. <http://hyakumonogatari.com>

INDEX OF YŌKAI